Nadja Schnetzler

The Idea Machine

Für Aaron Simpson

N. S.

Nadja Schnetzler

The Idea Machine

*How ideas
can be produced industrially*

WILEY-
VCH

WILEY-VCH Verlag GmbH & Co. KGaA

The original edition in German (*Die Ideenmaschine*) was published by Wiley-VCH Verlag GmbH & Co. KGaA in 2004. All rights reserved.

1st translated edition 2005

Library of Congress Card No.: Applied for

British Library Cataloguing-in-Publication Data:
A catalogue record for this book is available from the British Library.

Bibliographic information published by Die Deutsche Bibliothek
Die Deutsche Bibliothek lists this publication in the Deutsche Nationalbibliografie; detailed bibliographic data is available in the Internet at <http://dnb.ddb.de>.

© 2005 WILEY-VCH Verlag GmbH & Co. KGaA, Weinheim

All rights reserved (including those of translation into other languages). No part of this book may be reproduced in any form – nor transmitted or translated into machine language without written permission from the publishers. Registered names, trademarks, etc. used in this book, even when not specifically marked as such, are not to be considered unprotected by law.

Printed in the Federal Republic of Germany

Printed on acid-free paper

Typesetting   TypoDesign Hecker GmbH, Leimen
Printing and Bookbinding   Ebner & Spiegel GmbH, Ulm
Cover Design   init GmbH, Bielefeld

ISBN-13:   978-3-527-50135-9
ISBN-10:   3-527-50135-5

This book is dedicated to Markus:
Without you, there would be no Idea Machine

Love, Nadja

Contents

Foreword 9

Preface 11

Parking space for ideas 17

A machine produces ideas 21

Briefing & KickOff 39

CreatingCommunity 55

CreativeTeam 73

IdeaInterviews and ExpertInterviews 95

TrendScouting and NetScouting 109

IdeaCity and ThinkTank 121

IdeaDesign 137

IdeaSelection 153

IdeaManagement 167

Implementation 183

Parting words 193

Appendix 195

   Further reading and Web links 195

   The author 196

   The illustrator 197

   Index of persons 199

   Index of companies and brands 201

   Subject index 203

Foreword

We've all experienced it: For every invention there are a hundred experts who warn against it. When the printing press was invented, there were complaints about loss of aura and the threat of anonymity compared with the monks' personal documents; railways were seen as being dangerous for the human soul; the telephone was greeted with a great deal of scepticism, as people would no longer need to leave their homes and would become isolated and lonely. None of these things happened. The opportunities were always greater than the risks. If we had always listened to the hundred experts, then we would still be hungry and living in caves. Everything new and unheard of carries a certain risk. Every new development, every idea, has both positive and negative aspects; people only make progress by concentrating on the positive ones and developing them into significant strengths.

Good ideas don't just happen. You can block them or foster them. Nadja Schnetzler and her BrainStore are specialists at fostering them. They are familiar with the law of large numbers (pursue many ideas), lateral thinking (connecting apparently unconnected areas), failure tolerance (the fear of failure makes people into hesitators), dealing with "proven" innovation killers (arguments such as "we've always done it that way"), maintaining formal and informal communication and, of course, with all brainstorming techniques (producing ideas without rash criticism).

The implementation of such principles in companies and institutions still appears to be difficult and thinking in compartments is still widespread. Despite the fact that most innovations aren't even quantum leaps anymore: rather the result of the unexpected transfer of one pre-determined structure or practice onto another, the way we know and love it in the way children think and speak. People who only ever move on the heavily-used highways of normal association shouldn't be surprised when the variety of life on the unknown paths to the left and right passes them by...

It starts in kindergarten and primary school: originality and independent thinking need to be supported. Rash and superficial criticism, the alleged necessity of adapting to the known and normal, forcing children into an education system determined by the masses, will kill all enthusiasm for new things and experiments. Of course we need guidelines and principles: but standards and ideas aren't necessarily a contradiction in terms. In this book, Nadja Schnetzler shows, amongst other things, that the art of setting the right framework is the key to an unexpected idea. Excessive pressure for achievement in schools and the exaggerated "schoolification" of universities will never generate free spirits!

As individuals, we take all manner of high risks in extreme sports. Collectively however, everything is expected to be one hundred percent safe. That can't work in the case of innovations and obscures our view of their potential. Politicians and the administration need to demonstrate pleasure in innovation, risk and discovery. The will to reform in all essential areas should at least be able to be seen in the shining eyes of politicians, even if the implementation remains so difficult. Bill Gates' young garage company would have been prohibited by the factory inspectorate in Germany and polio vaccinations would never have been permitted today. We can no longer afford this kind of politics with its emphasis on warnings and prohibition. We need to hunger again for the new and the unusual in order to be able to enter the next millennium with self-confidence.

I hope this unusual book will help you to develop that hunger!

Munich, January 2004   Dr. *Florian Langenscheidt*

Preface

Inspiration is no substitute for hard work
Max Weber, German economist and social scientist (1864 – 1920)

No good architect would dream of rushing to put his inspiration for a new house into practice by immediately starting to build it. Before the building work can start, numerous planning and preparation stages are necessary. Drawings need to be made, the land needs to be surveyed, plans must be drawn up to exact tolerances, and, last but not least, the owners need to give their agreement to the proposed work, which often turns out to be the most difficult part of the whole process. An architect actually works in even more minute detail: without a clear commission and a detailed budget, he won't even start with the planning; he will first want to know what vision the other party has of his future dream home, what criteria are to apply and how much money can be spent.

What would be obvious to any five-year old in the example of building a house should also be valid for the search for new ideas in a company. However, things are quite different in reality: the search for ideas in a company often resembles a builder who orders the cement mixer and building workers before it is even clear what kind of building is to be built. Even worse: the first idea which comes up in a company is often taken to be good enough to commission complex research and start a whole engineering team off on an expensive implementation chain, only to possibly find out a few months later, that the idea wasn't that good after all and the project is then quietly buried.

Inspiration is no substitute for hard work. And inspiration not the same thing as a well thought out idea. Generating ideas, which are economically interesting and can also be put into practice, is a demanding and exacting process, although one which can be learned, a game with various players, rules and instruments. Only those who understand the principles of this game can be guaranteed to generate good ideas, both for new products and services and for internal challenges in the areas of processes, human resources management or strategy.

There has been a lot of talk about innovation and innovation management in the last few years. Many companies have sharpened their senses for the subject and are aware of how important innovation is for them. Some companies have defined processes and determined responsibilities for the development of innovations (primarily products and services). Unfortunately, these processes start too late. They rely on the fact that good ideas will be just lying around waiting to be fed into the processes.

But ideas don't just appear out of thin air. Sitting back and waiting to be hit by inspiration when looking for new ideas is like hunting for the famous needle in a haystack. Maybe you will have a stroke of luck in your search. Unfortunately, you will have bad luck more often than good luck, meaning you will often have to make do with an idea which neither meets the defined criteria nor is tailor-made for an existing problem. Luck and professionalism do not go together.

Every day, entrepreneurs ask themselves questions such as: how can I launch an industry trend? How can I immediately hit upon a brilliant idea? How can I use my company's resources to find ideas? How can I prevent the idea becoming a huge flop? Hundreds of books have been written on the subject of innovation, idea techniques, trends, suggested ways of going about it, criteria grids and so on. However, the thought that ideas could be developed systematically, i.e. that there could be a standardised process leading to successful, practicable ideas, is still highly unusual.

If you ask decision makers in industry how they come up with new ideas, then you get a range of very different answers. The most frequently cited methods are:

- Promote individual performance, often linked to a reward system or a suggestions scheme: the problem with this model is the rewarding of individual employees and the lack of acceptance by colleagues who were not part of the development. It has, however, been proved, that good ideas are created much more easily in a multidisciplinary team than by loners who, naturally, have a somewhat limited view of things. Wider support in the company is also worth its weight in gold in the implementation stage.

Therefore, well-meaning systems, such as company suggestions schemes, are often doomed to failure, because they do not encourage collective idea generation, but the hoarding of ideas and secrecy.
- A clever management, which discusses and develops ideas further in teams: the problem with this approach is the strong inward view – it is always the same people who are occupied always with the same idea. The subject is therefore only superficially exploited and unexpected solutions are rarely achieved. There is the additional danger of burnout with the core team.
- Ideas are linked to a certain manager: this is often the case in family-run companies, where the "patron" launches new ideas. This systems only functions as long as the manager concerned creates new ideas. If there is no efficient handover or no-one is let in on the secrets of this kind of idea generation, then the whole innovation power of the company – and thus the company itself – is at risk.

A clear, structured process for generating ideas is difficult to find in all of these methods. And yet company mission statements are still full of sentences such as "Our innovation power makes us market leaders …".

In some companies, several engineers work for months or even years on a single project (based on an idea) only to then establish that the idea doesn't hold what it promised. Valuable time for launching something new has been lost. Wouldn't it have been better to work on ten promising ideas in parallel for a limited time, to then see only some of them fail, whereas at least some of them would go on to become successful? Wouldn't it have been more interesting, to use the whole power of a research and development department for a few days, rather than have these clever people work alone for months?

A defined ideas process can find 10,000 seeds of ideas, from which 20 brilliant ideas are selected, which all go off in completely different directions (always focussed on the core task). Up to 1.000 people are included. The ideas are immediately tested in the market and input from different industry sectors and countries flow into the process. Stakeholders (customers, former customers, employees, suppliers) contribute to the idea. An idea which is developed in this way has wide support and you can start the implementation with a good feeling. And all of this costs significantly less than three top engineers who carry out research on a project for a year.

A determined, defined process for the development of ideas doesn't just serve to develop new products and services. An innovative company approaches every issue in an innovative way, regardless of whether it concerns an internal problem or the development of a new product.

Characteristics of innovative companies are: a love of experimentation, openness, the involvement of employees from all levels of the hierarchy, the inclusion of outsiders, the fostering of childlike curiosity and enjoyment of new things. In an innovative company, someone has been given responsibility for the development of ideas, clear processes exist for the development of new things (from the idea to implementation) and clearly allocated budgets are available for these projects. However, despite this clear assignment, every employee in the company is thought to be able to bring in new ideas.

Structures for innovation management must first be created and an idea generation culture must be consciously built up in the company. Structures, responsibilities, tools, rooms and procedures, criteria and frameworks are necessary to come up with good ideas, which can then be fed into the implementation pipeline. It may be necessary to include external partners who help to avoid tunnel vision.

In this book, you will get to know the parameters of successful idea generation. You will find out:

- how to approach idea development
- which players from inside and outside the company will be required
- how you should break down an idea task into details
- how you can search for a large number of ideas
- which methodology is suitable for it
- which filter processes should be used
- how good ideas can be shown and presented in a way which enables them to be compared
- which criteria are used in the decision process for the favourite idea

- how you can evaluate the quality of ideas
- which criteria are valid for this evaluation

And, you will have a great deal of fun in developing ideas at the same time. You can apply this process at any time to develop good, implementable ideas efficiently yourself.

***

By the way: you will not find that overused word "creativity" anywhere in this book.

If you would like to know a little more about any detail of industrial idea production at any point in this book, then give me a call or send me an e-mail:

Phone +41 79 251 11 56, e-mail nadja.schnetzler@brainstore.com

I wish you inspiring reading!

Biel, January 2005   *Nadja Schnetzler*

Parking space for ideas

Use this space to make a note of all ideas which occur to you when reading this book.

18 | Parking space for ideas

Parking space for ideas

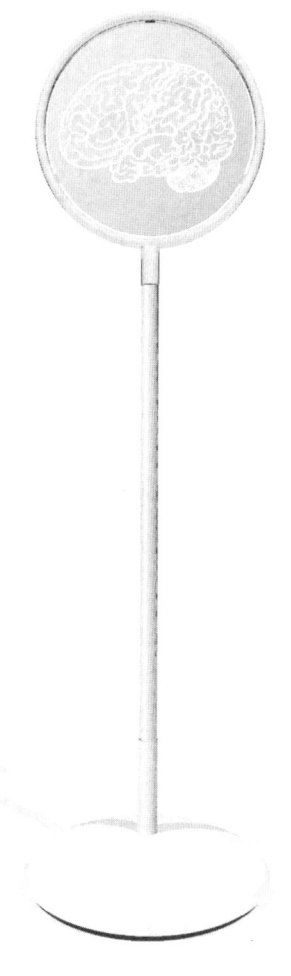

Parking space for ideas

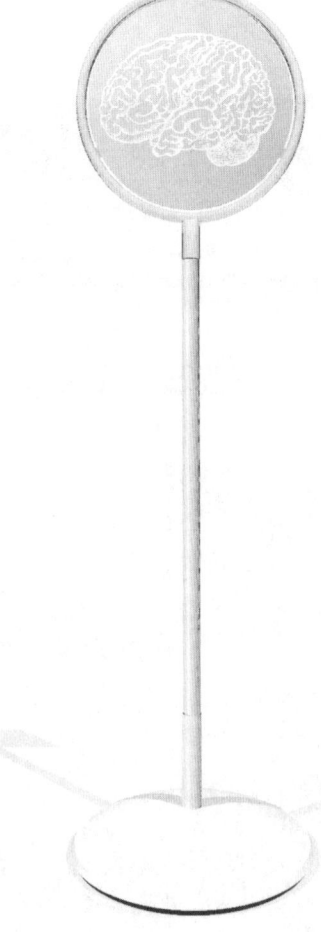

A machine produces ideas

Why industrial idea production makes sense.

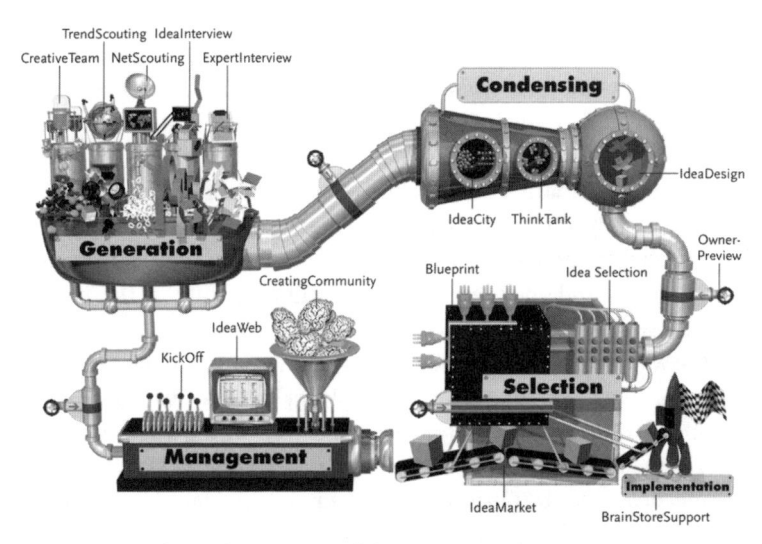

The BrainStore Idea Machine consists of idea generation, idea condensing, idea selection and implementation. In order for the machine to work, the idea process needs a cleverly devised idea management.

The word "idea" appears at least once in almost every film which has been made since the beginning of the 20th century,. One scene, which has to do with ideas, has particularly stuck out in my memory. It is from *Apollo 13* with Tom Hanks. The crew of Apollo 13 is stranded in space facing seemingly insurmountable difficulties and must move to the landing capsule, because all systems have crashed in the main room. As if that wasn't enough, the crew has problems with the CO^2 filters in the landing capsule. They are not working properly and are threatening the safety of the crew. At the same time, one of the most famous brainstorming sessions in history is taking place in Houston, when the flight leader calls together a team of specialists, empties a sack containing all the objects which are currently on board the Apollo 13 onto the table and says: "Build me a CO^2 filter as quickly as possible using these objects". The team gets to work and does what it does best: invent, invent, invent – until the solution has been found. Idea generation à la NASA; successful, yet by absolutely unsystematically in this case. What would have happened if their efforts had provided no meaningful solution?

Another scene comes from the film "Wag the Dog" with Dustin Hoffman and Robert de Niro, a parody of America in general and American politics in particular: immediately before the elections, the President needs to cover up an affair with an underage girl and therefore calls for his crisis manager (De Niro). Together with a Hollywood producer (Hoffman) and the President's domestic policy adviser (Anne Heche), the crisis manager stages a fictive war in Albania. When staging the virtual war, the team digs deep into Hollywood's box of tricks and cooks up an ideas soup according to the maxim "makes something new out of something old". A song is composed for the war, sung by the greats of the music industry, in the same way as the anti-hunger song *"We are the World"* several years ago, there are merchandising articles for the war, events for the war and heroes who allegedly return home from the war. The President's crisis team gets its best ideas by putting in nightshifts with vitamin pills and alcohol in the Hollywood producer's villa. Idea generation à la Hollywood.

Over the last few years, we have regularly asked our clients and partners how they generate ideas in their companies. Most of the people we asked are decision makers. We have collected over two hundred different answers. Amongst them were answers we had expected, for example "I do market research" or "my engineers are responsible for ideas in my company" or "I go abroad to find inspiration" or "I brainstorm with the management team", but also some which amazed us, such as "I go into a monastery", "I get my best ideas whilst driving" "My wife always gives me good ideas" or "when I look into the shaving mirror in the morning …".

Overall however, they have one thing in common: hardly any decision maker relies on a structured process: almost all of them rely on their own powers of inspiration or the powers of inspiration of other people. They all believe they must come up alone and spontaneously with good ideas which will drive their company forward. If these decision makers were not under time and innovation pressure, then these various idea generation techniques would certainly lead to acceptable results, as in "I'll go jogging for a few hours, that's when I always get my best ideas" What if however – and this is a realistic scenario - there is time and innovation pressure? The source of ideas which is otherwise so successful probably then provides no useful result.

A further disadvantage of individual idea generation techniques is that they are never supported by a broad base. No end-user was involved in the development of the idea, no expert could add his opinion to the idea generation process, no employee was integrated into the process. Such an idea can very quickly land in the electronic or physical waste paper basket because it has no relevance to a real need. And the decisive disadvantage is that not many different ideas generally result in this way, just one or two. What happens if none of these ideas can be implemented? Do you want to spend several more days jogging alone?

There are, of course, people who can create and implement fantastic ideas on their own. History provides numerous examples of the flashes of genius of single individuals. Art, music and the basic research in many scientific disciplines provide examples of ideas which really do need to develop without a systematic idea generation process. Van Gogh, Goethe, Mozart and Einstein didn't need an idea machine (they however were exceptional, highly inspired geniuses). In the lower levels of daily life, there are also examples of people or teams, which generate unsystematic, but nevertheless successful ideas every day.

There is an example of one such team right next to our idea factory in Biel: a small shop called "essor" (French for "upturn") which belongs to three friends of mine, who produce their own jewellery and also sell a small, exclusive collection of designer clothes, bags and accessories. Every month, the three face the question of how the shop window should be dressed for the next jewellery collection. They always choose a theme and then search for ideas on how to realise this theme in the shop window. Sometimes when I happen by, I'm included in their brainstorming, along the lines of "hey, you work in an idea factory, what occurs to you for our theme "Fools and their majesties?" I always enjoy these little discussions, because they are interesting and I learn a lot about how this team of three people creates its ideas. They develop ideas in the same way that most artistically talented people do. They discuss, discard, combine, argue, drink beer and finally agree on an acceptable path. If necessary, they include the opinion or ideas of some external parties. This method is highly unsystematic, but nonetheless leads to success. The shop windows are always surprising, interesting and present the jewellery in a way that makes you feel curious and want to enter the shop.

Other people, who don't have the same artistic potential as my three friends, aren't fortunate enough to come up with ideas in such an unsystematic and, really, ineffective way. Not everyone is a Leonardo da Vinci or a Marie Curie, who can create great things from within themselves. Quite apart from the fact that great things usually take time – and how many companies have time? A system is therefore needed, to produce ideas in a targeted way. And the good news is: it is actually relatively easy, to produce ideas systematically. So why carry on brooding, inventing and waiting for brilliant inspiration, when a systematic process can guarantee that you will develop a good, implementable idea in the desired time?

It's efficient to systematise the generation of ideas

Practically every action in a company is systematised: from the purchasing of raw materials, the production processes and delivery of goods, the setting up of a workplace, the ordering of material and the assessment of employees to the production of goods and marketing standards. Why is that so? Because it is efficient. And because this efficiency sets energy free for the things which are really important, for customer contact, for example. Only the search for ideas is carried out more or less unsystematically. It is actually the only part of the value chain which is still done in the same way that it was several hundred years ago, namely, by trial and error.

Most people think that only geniuses, artists or highly-paid specialists in a research and development department can develop ideas. That isn't the case. Good ideas can be developed in a short time if the right people are involved and if a structured process is adhered to. Additionally, the systematic search for ideas provides a sure path towards optimisation, which an individual person can never take: it's better to use the short time available to work with a variety of people in order to exploit the full potential of a subject and to evaluate all imaginable perspectives on the question and to then come to an acceptable and implementable result, than to take the risk that a genius will maybe find a solution on his own – or maybe he won't ... .

What does "industrial idea production" mean?

The principle of the industrial production of ideas is based on the thought that good ideas – whatever they are for – can be developed with a structured process, similar to other goods, which are produced according to a pre-determined process and using defined tools. That does not mean that the "old" forms of idea generation are no longer valid or no longer make sense. An artist will still create art on his own and from within, without having to use an idea generation process. And you can also wait for inspiration when you are not under time or success pressure. For all of those occasions in which this is not the case, our idea machine is one of a number of possible ways of systematically creating ideas. The principles behind the industrial production of ideas are independent from a specific process and are simply based on commonsense and many years of experience in the production of ideas.

The picture of the machine sums up the basic principles of the industrial production of ideas: ideas are developed in a clear, defined process and do not happen by chance. The machine always does the same thing, the individual steps are predefined. The machine can nevertheless be set for various tasks and it produces more than one variation; the result is always diverse ideas which meet all the requirements given.

This fact never ceases to amaze experienced engineers in particular, in companies such as Bosch/Siemens, Logitech, DuPont or Embraer (aircraft manufacture), who have produced ideas using our idea machine. An engineer is used to working on a scenario and "playing around" with a solution until he can book the project as a success or failure. The idea machine works in a completely different way: in the initial phase, it creates a structured mix of all the possible pieces of a jigsaw of a solution, condenses them in a second phase to possible scenarios and then works on five to twenty scenarios in parallel, which results in several projects always being able to be booked as successes – because they work. A further advantage of this procedure is the consistent inclusion of the IdeaTargets (e.g. customers, end-users, shareholders, employees, dealers, developers) in the idea generating process; in this way no innovations are developed which are not relevant for the market and is therefore liable to be rejected. In many technology-driven companies, the real cause for the failure of innovations is not the lack of innovation power, but the development of ideas which pass consumers by or are launched onto the market too early. WAP for example: this mobile phone technology, a forerunner of UMTS, is a technology with huge start-up difficulties. What would have happened, if the potential consumers had been involved in the development of the technology from the very beginning? It's quite likely that WAP and its applications would have greater acceptance today.

Generate – condense – decide

There is a very simple principle for the success of an idea generation project, which also describes the three most important components of the idea machine: generate ideas, condense ideas and select ideas. These three phases should become your personal mantra, a sentence which you always repeat when you set out on the search for ideas: generate, condense, select. It is vitally important that anyone who wants to develop ideas, separates these three phases from each other. First collect, then combine and refine, and only then decide. Sounds plausible, doesn't it? We think so, too. Nevertheless it is the most common and most serious stumbling block on the road to an idea.

I remember a brainstorming session in one of Switzerland's largest advertising agencies. I was invited as an outsider to search for a name for a car together with the agency people. I was curious how that would take place in such a well-known and respected agency and agreed immediately. Around eight people from the agency were present, with various functions, from the client advisor and the graphic designer to the person responsible for production. I was the only person from outside the agency; no-one was present form the client side. There was no introduction and no briefing. The only thing I was given was a picture of the new car, an estate, for which a name obviously had to be found. Okay, I thought, the others presumably know a lot about this car and don't need anymore detailed information. Let's wait and see.

The client advisor opened the brainstorming session with the words "So, any suggestions for a name for this car?" For about twenty seconds no-one said anything. Then, slowly, the first name suggestions came up, which the client advisor made a note of on the flipchart. As soon as the first suggestion was made, a discussion started on the sense, or lack of it, of that name and the brainstorming session drifted off into a fundamental discussion on the quality of names and the names of the client's other cars. After five minutes there were four names on the flipchart and none of them were good. The client advisor closed the meeting after a further ten minutes and a further three names on the flipchart and said she would think about the name some more together with the client.

A short analysis of this typical procedure from the point of view of the idea factory: What went wrong?

1. An unclear briefing. The participants didn't know what the session was about and didn't all have the same level of knowledge. The criteria and the task were not transparent.
2. The team consisted of a homogenous group of people who all had the same way of thinking (all people from the advertising agency). The client was not included, an outsider was, but only with an alibi function, because she had no access to the briefing or to information.
3. Lack of quantity. From a list of eight name suggestions, it is more or less impossible to choose a favourite which will be successful on the market. At least one thousand suggestions are needed to find a good name.
4. Instead of dividing the idea search into the phases of generation, condensing and decision, all phases were mixed up from the be-

ginning. The first idea was discussed and immediately destroyed by a destructive decision when the group was still in the collection phase. New ideas were never really given a chance.

Generate, condense, decide. Write that on your screen saver!

In the picture of the idea machine at the beginning of the chapter, you can clearly see that the phases are connected, yet still distinctly separate from each other. Once you have internalised this law, then you can enrich the phases with ideas:

- *Idea generation* using various techniques, for example, searching for seeds of ideas with insiders and outsiders, collecting desires and wants, user thoughts and needs in IdeaInterviews, asking experts, looking for inspiration in other countries or industry sectors or in the Internet (TrendScouting or NetScouting).
- *Condensing* ideas by constantly recombining the idea fragments generated in the generation phase, filtering the ideas which were gathered in an emotional scanning process, evaluating the ideas according to the criteria given in the briefing and developing final concepts, which are visually comparable.
- *Deciding* on the ideas in a structured form together with the ProjectOwner and the decision makers in the company.

According to our experience, what sounds easy here is a process which you must actively practice and take to heart. Even we, the idea factory workers, often fall into the same trap as our clients when we have to develop ideas for our own purpose. Probably because we think that something will occur to us in an unstructured way because we know about ourselves extremely well. Which, of course, it doesn't, the only things which come up are old ideas with a new look. And yet, you are constantly tempted to try the unsystematic approach, quite simply because you have the feeling that it's easier than a systematic approach. That is a fallacy however. Once you have got to know systematic working methods, then you come to appreciate the reliability of the results, the ease of working and the inclusion of insiders and outsiders in the project.

Insiders and outsiders collide

One of the most important laws of industrial idea production, is the necessity of a fresh, impartial perspective. You certainly won't achieve that if you approach idea generation alone or with your core team in the company. Instead, you need to include people with different backgrounds and perspectives in the idea generation process, and the potential users (IdeaTargets) of the idea also need to be included in the development at an early stage. In the chapter "CreatingCommunity" you will learn how to establish teams in the best way, what you need to consider when including outsiders and which outsiders we, as an idea factory, include in our clients' projects.

If you include the right people in the project, you've already achieved a lot. Forget the idea that only those people with expert knowledge on the subject at hand are of use in your idea generation projects. The more varied the areas of knowledge, specialism and interests in the project team in the idea generation phase, the better. Make interesting people part of your personal ideas network. You will find that all of these perspectives will be of use one day, quite apart from the enrichment which you will experience personally if you get to know and appreciate new and different people every day.

Idea generation

A simple formula: the less time there is available for the idea generation in total, the larger the number of inspirations you will need to collect to develop the idea. And the more time you have, the fewer initial ideas you will need, because the more time you can spend shaping them and you can also afford to wait for the decisive flash of inspiration. But: who really has the time to wait a long time for inspiration these days, when the market is calling for something new and the competitors are one step ahead again? We need, therefore, to find an excellent idea and to increase the initial chances in the short time available to us.

Take a big ladle to do the mixing. You will discard a lot of initial material, but the chance of happening on an interesting thought is considerably greater with a large quantity of "initial material" than with a few fragments. But what does that mean? We have a rule of thumb at BrainStore: a good idea needs at least 500 idea fragments. As you need at least six ideas, not one, to have one left at the end which you can select and implement, then you need at least 3,000 raw ideas or idea fragments, which you can then filter, combine and shape into ready ideas.

In order to find that much inspiration, you need, not only the right team (see chapter "CreatingCommunity"), but also the right tools. Roughly speaking, you have four basic possibilities for collecting inspiration. There is a separate chapter in this book on each of these possibilities:

- *CreativeTeams* are workshops of between one and six hours in which you collect raw materials together with insiders and outsiders.
- *TrendScouting and NetScouting* is the search for exotic, offbeat and unusual input from diverse industry sectors and countries, which you can include in the project at a later date.
- *ExpertInterviews* are discussions with experts who can give you raw ideas for certain ideas.
- *Idea Interviews* are surveys of employees, non-customers, management or other people, who could contribute something to the idea.

Condensing: from quantity to quality

Whereas in the first phase of idea production, you concentrate on the quantity, the variety of perspectives and the inclusion of different people, the second phase – condensing ideas – is concerned with drawing the right conclusions from the raw ideas which have been generated. This can be achieved most quickly if a suitable team of people specialised in methodology and content sort through and combine the raw ideas which have been found and reduce them to a number which is workable.

This again happens in various modules. The first part of the machine is called *IdeaCity*. Its function is to look at the idea fragments found in the idea generation phase and, with this perspective, to create new combinations and new ideas.

Then the *FirstScan* takes place, in which the ideas created in the IdeaCity are evaluated in an emotional way. It is decided whether an idea can remain in the selection, is rejected or should be changed in some way.

The next step is the *CriteriaScan*, in which the remaining ideas are evaluated based on the project criteria.

The ideas which are now left in the idea pot are fed into the *Think-Tank*, in which a small, skilled team of methodology and other specialists put the ideas through a thorough test in *Lava Lamping*. This technique has acquired its name because the ideas rise and sink, separate and join up as in the famous lava lamps from the sixties, which are now becoming popular again.

At the end of these (sometimes very heated and long) discussions, those ideas which have survived this endurance test are checked definitively for feasibility and implementability. After that, the ideas are formulated in simple language (able to be understood by a primary school child) and put into a comparable visual and content-related form in the *IdeaDesign* phase. In later chapters, you will learn in detail how all of these machine parts function and what you have to pay attention to if you want to develop ideas according to these principles yourself.

Making the decision process transparent

The ideas which are generated in the idea machine are good. You can rely on that. You cannot, however, always rely on the fact that everyone you present these ideas to will react objectively and constructively to them. Ideas are, above all, a matter of taste. A strong emotional component therefore comes into play. Emotions are, of course, a good thing in principle, ideas live from emotions. But it is important, that individual, perhaps irrelevant, emotional remarks do not destroy an idea from the outset.

It is therefore, vital that the decision process which leads to the selection of an idea be designed in a transparent way. This can be achieved at two levels. Firstly, by including the ProjectOwner (that is the person who commissioned the idea) into the project. This guarantees that the ideas do actually meet the needs of the company. The

ProjectOwners guide the project and make corrections to the course, if the project deviates too much from the objective. The Project Owners are also guarantors for good quality for the other decision makers in the company. Transparency is also achieved by presenting the finished idea to a generously defined group in the company and asking them to systematically evaluate it.

The *IdeaSelection* phase shows which ideas will be well accepted in the company, which will receive no agreement and which will have a strong polarisation effect. Ideas which have a polarisation effect are generally just as interesting as those which everyone thinks are good. Those ideas which have a polarisation effect within the company are usually those which also become the number one subject in the market. More information on this can be found in the chapter on "Idea Selection".

The selection of the ideas should be covered by a validation phase in the market, i.e. by those persons who will actually use the idea. The market should, however, never be confronted by more than three variations, and these should have already been given wide agreement from within the company.

Idea Management

The industrial production of ideas is so appealing, because for each project those people who are best suited to it can be involved in each case and can bring their skills and their expert knowledge to the project. This means however, that the management and control of the project is demanding. And it also means that the idea management takes on a role which is, above all, a coordination role and does not necessarily produce the ideas itself. The ideas management is, of course, also responsible for the content-related quality, but it essentially ensures this by making sure that the framework for idea production functions and that the right people have the right tools available at the right time in order to be able to develop ideas. This leads to irresistible efficiency.

Many potential employees of our idea factory are therefore disappointed at first when they learn that their role in the idea factory will involve much more coordination and planning than creative work on ideas. Those who believe that you can really express yourself and put your ideas into action in an idea factory, have the wrong image of idea management. But no good ideas can be developed without a coordination function and someone who has methodological knowledge and an overview of the idea project. Idea management involves developing a clear project briefing together with the ProjectOwner (chapter "Briefing and KickOff"), quality monitoring of the project, looking after the ProjectOwner, critically examining processes, ideas and concepts and the presentation and driving of an idea project. More on this subject can be read in the chapter "IdeaManagement".

Implementation

Implementation is the logical consequence of a good idea. Nevertheless, many good ideas spend too much time in the drawer and are therefore old hat by the time they are to be implemented. The timing of the implementation is critical for the success of an idea, and must already be taken into consideration in the development of the project briefing.

Of decisive importance is the early, but not too early, inclusion into the project of those who will potentially be involved in the implementation. The foundations for the implementation work already need to be laid early in the condensing phase of idea generation, by thinking through feasibility, required resources, what-happens-if questions and various scenarios. The weighting of these questions will vary depending on the urgency of implementation.

If, for example, you are looking for visions for possible commodity products in ten years time, then implementation is not the most urgent issue. If however, you are planning an event which is to take place in three weeks time, then questions concerning implementation are of central importance. More hints on this subject can be found in the chapter "Implementation".

The industrial Production of Ideas
– a sector gains in importance

15 years ago, we, two students and a girl at grammar school, established our company. Our simple idea was to bring together young people who have ideas and companies who need ideas. At that point in time, we had no idea that the process of industrial idea production would develop out of it. We did, however, know that we had found a basic mechanism for producing ideas, which is amazingly simple: the systematic bringing together of insiders and outsiders released energy and dynamics for new ideas, which we had never imagined. As a very young team, our first projects were in the youth area; we developed ideas, for example, for a new Coca-Cola campaign, a new snack product or ideas on how to make young people aware of the subject of not smoking. Our methodology was rather homemade and not highly developed, but the bringing together of insiders and outsiders was love at first sight. In the project for the Swiss Health Authority, in which young people were to be motivated to be voluntarily vaccinated against hepatitis B, young people from all over Switzerland came together with highly-specialised doctors to develop and discuss ideas. We observed how the two sides spontaneously and quickly came close to each other. The young people had a lot of questions concerning hepatitis B and the doctors had a lot of questions for the young people. Through skilful moderation, we achieved a situation in which both sides enriched each other and a good idea was developed for a campaign which both convinced the young people and was of value to the Health Authority.

This and a number of other experiences from the early days of BrainStore showed us that this formula of bringing insiders from the company together with very young outsiders, works. It's like a good soup: if the right ingredients come together, then it simply tastes better. And every attempt we made at diverting from this basic principle didn't work, for example, when we took on students from the subject area of the client instead of teenagers or, for budget reasons, only worked with insiders; these experiments just didn't bring the same level of good ideas as our insider/outsider mix.

From this basic mechanism, further tools and techniques were developed over the years, to develop ideas quickly and reliably and with guaranteed acceptance by the decision makers involved in the project. We only added the label "Industrial Idea Production" after we understood that we had found a key to producing ideas in the same way that other products are produced: with a machine. New parts were added to this machine over time, the interfaces were and are constantly checked, und their functioning improves and becomes more reliable.

Many of the machine parts which we take for granted nowadays only exist because of special client projects: with every new invention project new techniques, tools and improvements were added which we were trying out for a client – nothing unusual for an idea factory, every commission is new ground for use in some way. We are used to looking at every task with the carefree and curious view of a child and let ourselves be surprised by where the task will lead us.

It was new territory for us, for example, when Johnson & Johnson asked us to develop new ideas with young women in Switzerland for the promotion of panty liners. We knew nothing about market research, in the same way that we know nothing about most of the subjects which clients ask us to deal with. This forces us to think about subject area and get to know it more quickly, thoroughly and pragmatically. A very important part of our idea machine developed from this first market research project, namely the components for very targeted idea and expert interviews, which can be evaluated in relation to the idea project.

The enormous amount of time and effort we used to build up a market research unit for the first time for our client Johnson & Johnson, has paid for itself a hundred times over since then, because we can now offer other clients a tool to better support their innovation projects. Every tool and every machine part which we regularly use for our clients has been checked and reworked many times over. An ideas machine is not something static: it is in a constant state of development, it is given new parts, tools fuse, become more refined or are replaced by newer versions. Every technique we try out and find good, goes through several testing stations in our development before it can be integrated into the idea machine. You can therefore be sure that the principles, tools and concepts which I suggest in this book are not simply nice ideas, dubious experiments or abstract ideas far removed from practice. The idea machine has proved its validity – in hundreds of "serious" projects.

When we first presented our current idea machine to companies in 1997, we were not aware how revolutionary the idea was. To us, it was simply the logical steps from disconnected tools on the subject of innovation to a systematic, industrial process from which clients in all industry sectors could benefit equally. The *Neue Zürcher Zeitung* wrote about BrainStore in 1999 as if it were a company from the twenty-first century.

At that point in time, innovation and the generation of ideas was pretty much neglected in the majority of companies. There were no signs of a Chief Innovation Officer as can occasionally be found today. Innovation was limited to the development of products and services, and this development was either driven by marketing alone or was the responsibility of a research and development department.

But innovation is a subject which doesn't stop at other areas of the company. Really innovative companies not only have innovative products and an innovative image, but see innovation as the motor of the whole company. They are driven by the thought "How can we do it even better?" and this applies to all areas, from the search for new employees or customer service to the food in the canteen. Innovative companies see their activities as an adventure, as an expedition into unknown territory and not as the linear fulfilment of duty in a certain industry sector, in which best practice is already prescribed. Innovative companies like to make decisions, have hierarchies which are as flat as possible and constantly involve their employees in the further development of the company. Such companies already follow the central principles of the industrial production of ideas such as the inclusion of multidisciplinary teams, clear structures and processes for the generation of ideas and the implementation of ideas as well as an integrated, company-wide attitude towards innovation.

But what they are missing is the machine which enables them to develop the ideas they need quickly and reliably. With such a machine, they would be in a position to develop their own ideas very quickly. But even those companies which are not innovative to the core need new ideas every day. Their success depends decisively on whether or not they can differentiate themselves from the products and services of their competitors. Differentiation is becoming increasingly difficult. There are only a limited number of differentiation possibilities at the level of pricing, at the product level good ideas tend to be copied, and at the marketing level most companies use the same basic ideas. This means that companies need to fight for differentiation at all levels. They need ideas for this on a daily basis. Anyone who wants to develop these ideas without huge personnel and time resources needs a system a process, or, simply: an idea machine.

Core Concepts "The industrial production of ideas"

- The industrial production of ideas is a relatively new concept. The generation of ideas still takes place in an unsystematic and manual manner in many companies. But it is possible to produce ideas just as systematically as any other product.
- There are numerous techniques and procedures for coming up with ideas. But most of them are only suitable when enough time and inspiration is available. In all other cases they fail because they rely on the inspiration of individuals.
- The pressure on companies to innovate is increasing; differentiation is only possible with good ideas at all levels of the company.
- The industrial production of ideas includes people from within the organisation, outsiders and the potential users of the idea, i.e. the market, in the process.
- The industrial production of ideas is efficient and enables the development of a good idea in a clearly defined timeframe, at clearly defined costs, including all relevant perspectives and decision-makers.
- The idea machine for the production of ideas comprises various parts: idea generation, idea condensing, idea selection and implementation. These phases must be clearly separated from each other, even in small, simple idea projects. In order to operate the machine, the process needs to be controlled and guided (ideas management).

Briefing & KickOff

You can only find something, if you know what you're looking for

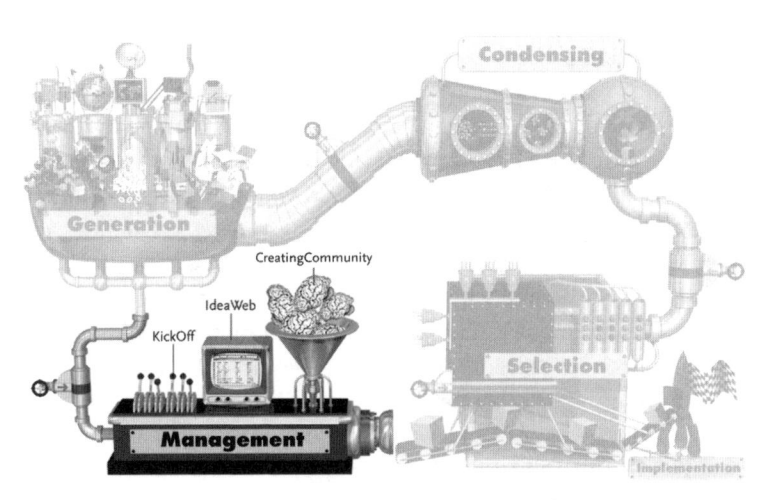

Briefing and KickOff are phases in idea management. They define in detail what the idea project is about, what the objectives are, which criteria need to be considered and how the idea generation project should be carried out. Idea production can only start once these points have been very clearly defined.

"We need a new product in our range. Who has a good idea?" said the manager of a Swiss brand of chocolate to his team. One person in the team asked if there were any framework conditions or criteria for the intended new product. The manager's answer was very typical "I don't want to limit you unnecessarily at this stage. Just come up with something". The meeting ends and the teams sets off on the search for the Holy Grail like a bunch of drowned rats. And they don't even have a map.

Many managers believe that a rudimentary formulation of the question is enough to search for good ideas and that the fewer the conditions attached, the less a team is "limited", then the better the ideas will be. They believe that total freedom is much more inspiring than a focussed search. That is a fallacy. Even people who know the company well and are aware of both the company culture and its strategic challenges will hardly develop convincing ideas based on such a question formulation. The formulation of the question is simply too general and too wide and there is no background information or criteria provided – quite apart from the fact that the search simply by thinking is considerably more ineffective than a structured idea generation process.

It sounds paradoxical, but the more interesting the idea needs to be, the more clearly the playing field needs to be marked out from the beginning. Once I know the playing field, then I can move freely in it and explore all its limits. If the field is not marked out, then I don't know where to start looking for ideas, so many possibilities are open to me. It's like with a child who has no limits set: it will not develop as well as a child who knows where the boundaries of its behaviour are. Or to put it another way: I need a map with which I can start to search for treasure. Orientation points, information on direction und impenetrable thickets, mountains and taboo oceans are indicated on the map. In this way, the search for the treasure doesn't resemble the infamous search for the needle in a haystack.

A good idea generation project moves between structure and chaos. A structured briefing is only of value, if you let yourself be inspired by it in the idea collection phase (see chapters "CreativeTeam", "IdeaInterview" and "TrendScouting") and use it to the full. For this, you also need to be able to allow ideas which are completely ridiculous – within the given corridor. The limitations make clear in which direction the relevant ideas are likely to be found.

Marking out the field

So we're looking, for example, for a new chocolate product. The persons responsible, the ProjectOwners, need to consider in detail in advance of the idea generation process, what they are actually looking for, based on the existing products, the competition's products and the company's possibilities. You need to have an "idea" of the direction in which the idea could go. If, for example, the chocolate company is confronted with an audience which is too old, then it could make sense to develop a product which would address a younger audience – or vice versa. "What are we actually in a position to manufacture?" could be a second possible question. Is it thinkable to acquire a new machine or production plant based on the new product ideas or would that break the budget? What would be a good time to introduce the new product, i.e. how quickly would the new idea need to be implemented? What is the available research and development budget for the new product? For example, can the company afford an expensive laboratory phase in which a product with completely new characteristics such as consistency or aroma is developed? Which products were particularly successful in recent years and which were not? Is market data available, which provides information on the chocolate eating habits of consumers? Which raw materials/ingredients are taboo, which are wanted? Which other criteria does the product need to meet? Which existing company brand could be used as a vehicle for the new product? Or would it make sense to look for a completely new brand? These are just some of the possible questions which need to be answered in advance of the idea search.

Unclear instructions lead to unclear ideas

If the field has not be clearly marked out for the idea search, then it won't be possible to find good ideas. Criteria, budget levels, taboos and company culture give a good framework for the search. And the better you know what is definitely not wanted, the better you can define subject fields in which you can romp around. If, for example, I know that the children's help organisation only has 150.000 Euro available for the new campaign next year, then I will look for completely different subjects and ideas than if I didn't have this information. Even worse: if this basis is not available to me, then I will possibly develop ideas which are completely unrealistic and cannot be implemented.

The managers of MindLab in Copenhagen, a ThinkTank for the Economics Department of the Danish Government have told me that they often have to question the entire formulation of their clients' question. This is the case because it concerns particularly complex projects which cannot be transferred 1:1 to the idea generation process. One project for example, concerned the subject "economic growth in Denmark". It is a major challenge to find a clear formulation of this issue which all those involved with the project can agree on. Firstly, everyone needs to be clear what they mean by "growth" and which parameters can be changed in future (conditions for companies, laws, social and cultural attitudes ...). This common platform needs to be established before you can start looking for ideas. The more interested parties you have, as in the example of governments, the more demanding it will obviously be to find a common platform. But it's always worth doing the work, because this enables misunderstandings to be avoided in the project.

A thousand and one "stupid" questions

When we start a new project, we organise a kick-off meeting with our clients, a start-up meeting for the idea generation project. It serves to clarify all existing questions concerning the idea generation. As outsiders, who usually know little about the company and its culture, it also provides us with an opportunity to get to know the company's activities as well as possible. In some cases, we additionally spend a few days in the company in order to properly understand what they are currently working on. In the kick-off meeting we ask a lot of questions and we question a lot of things. We approach the project in a quasi journalistic way. The more we ask, the more we learn.

As outsiders, we obviously have the privilege of being able to ask "stupid" questions, because we do not know the activities and problems of our clients particularly well at that time. (NB: we obviously don't ask the really stupid questions until we have received the idea generation commission ...) we have noticed that it is often these apparently stupid questions which provide the most information about the project – a fact which you should take into consideration in your idea projects. Why not discuss the briefing with someone you trust from outside the company? You'll be amazed how many questions you will hear which will help you to formulate your question.

It is also often extremely exciting and amusing for outsiders to occupy themselves with the formulation of questions for idea generation. As an idea factory we come into contact with intimate information on our clients and get to know many different company cultures every day, quite apart from the extremely wide industry sector knowledge which we have acquired during the 14 years of our business activity. Our client portfolio includes sectors from virtually every letter of the alphabet: aeronautics, aerospace, aromas, banks, cars, chemicals, dentists supplies, discount stores, drinks, earthquake-proof buildings, food, functional food, herbicides, home electronics, hospitals, insurance, interest groups, investment goods, media, office material, perfume, political parties, prevention campaigns, private individuals, public transport, quartz watches, radio channels, retail, telecommunications, television, tools, yoga centres, youth products and many others. This wide sector knowledge is useful for every new project, because we can always draw parallels to sectors we already know. Nevertheless, as outsiders we are free from cumbersome detailed knowledge, prejudices, predefined thought trails and company taboos. Additionally, we are more free concerning our appearance to the client because of our specialised activity of the generation of ideas; no-one expects standard consultants in black suits and expensive watches on their wrists from us.

The better we can get a feeling for the way our clients "tick" in the KickOff, the better we can accompany them through the idea generation project and adapt to their peculiarities, special wishes and "offbeat" sides. Our client Syngenta for example, a leading agricultural business, needs to be able to coordinate innumerable international project leaders and decision-makers for every idea generation project. It can quite easily happen, that we spend the first hour of a KickOff meeting, deciding on a suitable location for the idea generation project, which then ends in a heated, amusing discussion on the advantages and disadvantages of various international airports. In the next project, we can include this client-specific knowledge directly into the KickOff meeting and suggest a solution which is suitable for the client: "Robert, what do think of London? As a matter of fact, we've discovered a new shop in the airport, which you would like and found a hotel which is within a hour of the airport"

In other cases, we notice how much our clients identify themselves with their products and how little they realise that this identification can seem somewhat absurd to outsiders. A leading manufacturer of toilet systems for example, loudly talked during the meal after our KickOff meeting about the benefits of this and that toilet, about small and big "jobs" and about the problems some of their customers have with their toilets. As you can imagine, we had more difficulties in "submerging ourselves" in this subject than in all others cases. However, once we have thoroughly occupied ourselves with a topic, then we also start to behave in the same way as our clients, and it is quite likely that we start to talk intensively about toilets and their benefits and disadvantages on all suitable and unsuitable occasions.

In any case, the question of distance is an important subject, particularly at the beginning of the idea generation process. Somewhere between a blinkered attitude to the company and its products on the one hand and a lack of interest on the other, there is a mental and emotional state of mind which is ideal for constructively "questioning the validity" of the project. You only have to ensure that you can get those involved in the project into this state of mind. The outsiders you bring into the project will be of valuable service in this.

A common language leads to better results

As a result of the KickOff meeting, the question for the idea generation project is formulated in such a way that everyone is in agreement about the direction which the idea we are looking for should go in. Our task as an idea factory is to guarantee that the question formulation actually makes sense, because a really good idea can only be developed with a question formulation which makes sense. This can be very hard work.

I remember an example where we were supposed to develop a new slogan for MediaMarkt Switzerland. The Marketing Manager and the Store Manager were present at the kick-off meeting. When it came to determining the criteria for the new slogan, the two of them could not agree whether the main statement should be "wide selection" or "low price". The two of them suggested that both statements be given equal value. We at BrainStore were against this, there is no such thing as a slogan in which two statements which are equally important, and we would have disappointed one of them. We spent around two hours in this room and asked a lot of questions to find out how the statements should be prioritised. We agreed on "wide selection" as the main criterion and defined "low price" as an ancillary criterion. The final slogan was in Swiss German: "Luege, lose, chaufe" meaning: look around, hear other opinions, and then purchase, a variation on the rhyme children learn in kindergarten in Switzerland for road safety "luege, lose, laufe" (look left and right, listen, then cross the road).

In workshops with companies which would like to learn how to develop idea briefings, I have established that most people have a lot of difficulty in separating the preparation for generating an idea from the actual idea generation. They start immediately with the search for ideas and run, so to speak, into the first available dead end. In order to help to separate the preparation and the actual search for ideas, I have introduced the "parking space for ideas" into these workshops. As soon as someone deviates and starts to describe an idea, the other participants ask him to write this idea in the parking space for ideas. The two phases can thus be clearly separated from each other. These ideas can then be fed into the total spectrum of ideas at the right time, namely in the idea generation phase. While we're on the subject: if a few ideas occur to you whilst you are reading this book, then please don't put the book aside to start immediately with the realisation. We have included a parking space for ideas for you at the beginning of the book for that purpose. Make a note there of your thoughts for later, relax again and continue reading ... .

The Briefing – short and using easy language

The briefing for the idea generation process is not written by the client in our projects, but by us, as a kind of "receipt" so that he can check that we have understood him correctly. You can also use this principle in internal projects by having the idea generation team write the briefing as the result of the KickOff. The internal "client" concerned should be present at the KickOff and subsequently confirm the briefing. This will ensure that the results will really be relevant later.

The briefing is very simply structured and usually consists of no more than three pages. The first page describes the initial situation in which the client currently finds himself. What is it really about, which issues occupy the client at that time? On the second page, we talk about the objectives of the idea generation. There we define exactly what we are looking for, how the central question is formulated, which main criterion is valid for the search for ideas and which ancillary criteria are important (no more than two ancillary criteria). Additionally, we describe exactly how many ideas the client can expect at the end of the idea generation process. All of this information should be short, sharp and to the point and be able to be understood without any insider knowledge. Our test: if a twelve year old can repeat the essence of the briefing after reading it once, then the briefing is clear.

Example of a good briefing (slightly shortened):

Initial situation
The foundation Mine-Ex has set itself the objective of helping victims of landmines all over the world and at the same time of lobbying for the removal of landmines. As every year, the foundation is holding a charity gala which has two objectives, namely collecting money on the one hand, and forcefully making people aware of the subject of landmines on the other hand.

Objectives
The foundation is now looking for good ideas for the next gala, to make the visitors remember it.

Criteria
The main criterion for the idea to be looked for is large public resonance. People should talk about the foundation.
　　Secondary criteria for the ideas are a) the largest possible fundraising success at the charity gala and b) idea which can be implemented for a maximum of 15,000 euros.

Results
At least five ideas are to be presented for activities which would have a significant public effect.

From this point on, this briefing (simplified and shortened here) is our compass through the entire idea generation project. It serves as a basis for all work steps and is read and consulted over and over again. If the briefing is good and clear, then there is no reason for questions and it is a good signpost. If it is unclear or shoddily formulated, then you will repeatedly stumble in this idea generation process and be unable to agree on objectives and criteria. An unclear briefing really can bring the whole idea generation to a standstill, because you repeatedly have to occupy yourself with the question of what it is all about.

A good briefing is particularly important when outsiders are included in the process. A good briefing brings the most important points to an understandable level for the outsiders and thus ensures that everyone speaks the same language.

Clear briefings need practice

You need to practice preparing a good briefing. That also applies to us at BrainStore. We've found an ideal practice field: we practice it with private individuals. We've set up an ideas shop, in which private individuals can commission an idea for around 10 euros. We write a briefing with them and then carry out a short but intensive idea generation process ("power brainstorming"). Private individuals are good practice clients for writing briefings because they, as opposed to company employees, are not generally used to formulating any kind of commission (that many company employees do it daily and are still not good at it, is another story).

Dealing with private individuals requires a very sensitive approach as it concerns private questions. Nevertheless, it is important to ask as many questions as possible it order to be able to clearly mark out the field. Therefore, if a man asks what he could give his girlfriend as a birthday present, you have to ask him what his girlfriend likes, what she doesn't like, what he gave her last year, how much he wants to spend, if he would be prepared to make or do something himself, etc. In order to get answers to the questions, you need to ask in a much more targeted and persistent way than with companies. And you need to check just as closely whether the question makes sense as it is formulated. There are, namely, private individuals who come to us under false pretexts and actually need something completely different. There was, for example, an elderly lady who came to us in the ideas shop and said she was hearing funny noises in her kitchen and wanted to know what she could do about it. A project manager wrote the briefing with her over a cup of coffee, asked her a few directed questions and it transpired that the noises in the kitchen were only a secondary problem, the "real" problem was at home in the living room, had been married to her for decades, had retired a month earlier, didn't know what to do with himself and was seriously getting on her nerves. He didn't even want to investigate the funny noises in the kitchen .... We developed some ideas for her on how she could get her husband interested in something again.

Unbelievable idea commissions

We love these private commissions in our ideas shop. The range of questions we have already been confronted with is unbelievable. There was someone who worked in a museum, who felt himself to be ignored by his boss and wanted to know how he could get more recognition from him. There was the twelve year old boy who wanted to persuade his father to buy him a computer; the offspring of a Greek shipping dynasty who was looking for an appropriate name for his chalet in Switzerland; the 75-year old lady who wanted to fall in love again; the parents looking for a memorable ceremony for their child's christening; or the father of three daughters with telephonitis who wanted to get a grip of the cost problem once and for all.

The work with private individuals constantly gives us new ideas as to which companies could possibly need ideas. There was, for example the dog-owner who wanted to make an advent calendar for her little darling and asked us for some ideas on what it could look like and how it could function. We found the question so interesting that we immediately contacted a large manufacturer of pet food and developed new ideas for pet products with them. We obviously would not present the ideas which we developed with a private individual to a company, that's a matter of honour. But the question permits a

Private individuals confront us every day with questions for ideas which range from the funny to the serious and help us to constantly improve our process.

Unbelievable idea commissions | 49

business application, along the lines of: everyone who is looking for an idea also brings us one.

Our work with private individuals also has further advantages for us: using simple tasks we can constantly monitor the idea generation process and fine-tune it. Or it becomes possible to test new tools and procedures in a "playful" arena. Last but not least, the projects with private individuals are the only area in which future idea producers can practice; unfortunately you cannot study idea production at a university or learn it in an apprenticeship. Not yet, but who knows, in 1950, there was no such thing as a computer scientist ... .

Briefing is a top management task

You cannot delegate an idea briefing. It is vital that the person who finally decides which idea will be implemented be involved in the preparation of the briefing. The reasons are simple: if someone is not involved in the briefing for the idea generation, then he will not be able to evaluate the quality of the final ideas. If, however, the decision-maker has the opportunity of determining the quality criteria at the beginning, then he will also be able to objectively evaluate the quality at the end.

We know enough clients who want to avoid responsibility for the briefing. In most cases we can persuade them to take part in the briefing using sensitive argumentation and bad examples from the past. We make it clear to them that the client is spending good money for a process which produces ideas tailored to a specific briefing and that it would be, not only a pity, but also stupid not to take the opportunity of ensuring that not just any old ideas are produced but the right ones.

Those projects which we, against our better judgment, have carried out without this level of involvement by the decision-makers have always produced less satisfactory results than those in which the criteria and objectives were worked out in agreement with those who make the decisions. It is not enough for the decision-maker just to deliver his input to the project (which he does anyway if the project is important to him). He must be involved in the preparation of the briefing, be present at the KickOff and read and approve the written briefing which was prepared. This is the only way to avoid misunderstandings and incorrect interpretations.

Even when all these steps have been followed in detail, there is still no guarantee that everyone is really talking about the same thing. Even in projects which have been well-prepared it can happen that individual participants have a different view of the kind of idea to be looked for than other project participants. It is therefore, useful if the briefing is regularly consulted. The project manager needs to repeat it until everyone knows what the idea search map looks like.

I remember an idea generation project for Migros, Switzerland's largest retailer. In this project, ideas were supposed to be developed as to how the company's employees could transfer the motto "freshness" to customers and other employees as the central theme of the company. The briefing had been determined and was clear and we were ready for the first CreativeTeam, in which Migros employees would search for ideas together with BrainStore and outsiders. Then the ProjectOwner, the person who had commissioned us, had another important appointment at the last minute and sent someone else to the workshop. The problem was that she didn't know the briefing and was, therefore, unprepared. When we went through the briefing together in the start-up meeting, the representative suddenly said "No, that's completely wrong! That's not the idea we're looking for!". This statement came at the wrong time and unsettled all other participants. We needed over an hour to discuss the briefing together and to clarify the fact that the project had been commissioned in that way and no other way by the boss and then we could finally start with the CreativeTeam.

A briefing can develop

A briefing can, of course, change or develop further during an idea generation project. But, each of these changes to the briefing needs to be considered carefully and, above all, needs to be clearly recorded. A change of course can sometimes make sense, for example, if new strategic considerations are brought into play, if the budget develops or if new knowledge changes the briefing. In such cases, it also needs to be clearly recorded what will change in the entire idea generation process with regard to working steps used, tools, participants and timeframe.

It starts to become dangerous when the idea search changes completely within a project. Experience shows that this happens in most cases if the project management changes and the objectives are defined in a completely new way. In this case, it needs to be carefully considered whether it still makes sense to continue with the project under these changed conditions or whether it might be better to start from scratch again. The risk that a new project management has completely different objectives than the old one is high. In such a case therefore, it is likely that any existing briefing will no longer be relevant.

Breaking down the briefing

Unfortunately, a good briefing isn't the end of it. It would be impossible to answer the question "What would be a good idea for a new chocolate product?" in that form in an idea generation process. This question, as banal as it may seem, is much too complex for an idea search. The question needs to be broken down into its component parts and define various perspectives from which it can be viewed. These search fields can be very adventurous and offbeat. What is important is that they are as concrete as possible so that the participants in the idea generation process can immediately work with the question. Some examples:

- "What would be a great kind of chocolate for senior citizens, business people, babies, mars men, technology junkies, giraffes, designers, nurses, people who hate chocolate, chocolate addicts ... ?"
- "What new ingredients can you add to chocolate?"
- "On which occasions could more chocolate be eaten?"
- "Chocolate makes people happy. What other additional functions could chocolate have?"
- "Healthy chocolate – how about that?"
- "With which new products could you entice people who don't really like sweet things?"

- "What kind of chocolate products exist in other countries, but not here?"
- "How could smokers be persuaded to change to chocolate?"

You will use this kind of concrete "small" questions during the project rather than "big" questions", whether it is in CreativeTeams, in surveys, in TrendScouting or in NetScouting. As a rule of thumb: the more complex the project, the more it needs to be broken down and the more time will be needed to generate ideas (more information on this in the Chapter "CreativeTeam").

Thinking into the future

At the beginning, you will probably have difficulty in breaking down the complex question formulation and isolating separate concrete questions. One particular risk is that people generally prefer to occupy themselves with the past rather than the future. It serves little purpose therefore, if for the question "How do we get more people into our store", you consider why the customers don't come today or didn't come yesterday, what you are doing wrong in the store and why the wrong people come to you. It's much better to formulate positive questions:

- "What steps can we take in our store to make it more interesting for customers?"
- "What does the absolute dream store for a shopaholic look like?"
- "In which store do people who hate shopping even feel good?"
- "What can we do outside the store to attract people?"
- "What promotions can we do to get people into the store?"

As you can see, the point is to identify all possible scenes for the idea and formulate simple questions for it. In the example of the store, it obviously makes particular sense if you visit the store together with the participants in the idea generation process and generate ideas there. It will also be necessary to prepare questions for this purpose: it is very important that all sub-questions – as with the briefing – are very, very simple and concrete. You need to filter even very complex questions to the extent that a child would understand the sub-questions. Only then can you close the briefing and KickOff phase and develop the next phase productively based on the work which has been done.

Core Concepts "Briefing and KickOff"

- The briefing is top management's responsibility. Make sure that the decision maker(s) who will finally judge the idea, are involved in the preparation or, at least, the evaluation of the briefing.
- Set aside enough time at the beginning of an idea project to clearly formulate the question for the idea search. Include all necessary persons who can contribute something. Let an outsider question the briefing.
- The briefing should not be longer than three A4 pages. You can add additional reading material, but the core briefing should be short. It comprises the initial situation, the objectives for the idea with the main criterion and possibly two ancillary criteria as well as the expected results (how many ideas in what form).
- Define the objective of the idea, if possible, without using the word "and" in your sentence.
- Define absolutely clear criteria. But do not define too many; one main criterion and two ancillary criteria are sufficient.
- Do the test: does a twelve-year old child you know understand what it's about? If so, then you can go ahead.
- Use the briefing as a working paper and daily companion in the idea generation project. Make sure that all persons involved in the idea generation project also know the briefing and know that it represents a consensus of the project participants. Make a record of changes and modified objectives in the briefing and always work with the current version.
- When you have a good briefing, start to break it down into search fields and sub-questions. Include as many different perspectives as possible and formulate simple and concrete questions for these perspectives, which you can later use when looking for inspiration. Formulate positive, open questions. The same principle also applies here: the simpler the question, the better the expected ideas will be. For simple questions, four to six sub-questions are enough for an idea search, for relatively complex questions around ten to fifteen, and for highly complex questions, twenty to thirty sub-questions.

CreatingCommunity

*Sharing your ideas
with others makes
them more valuable*

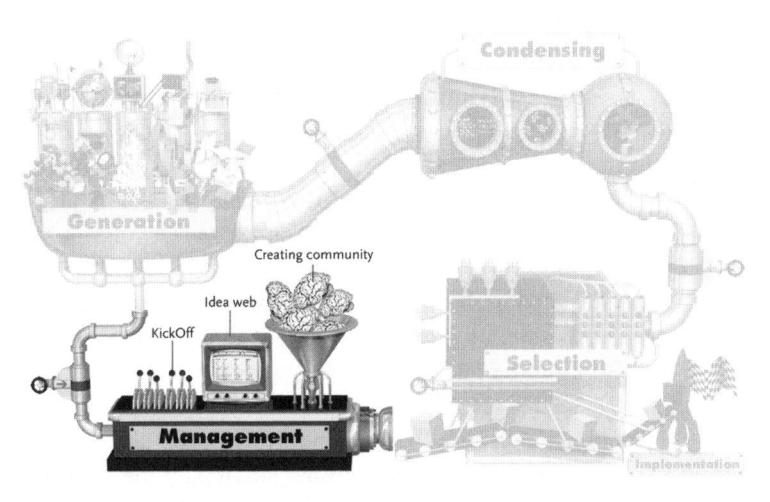

In order for your idea machine to function, you need to get the right people on board. The CreatingCommunity is a group of people, made up of insiders and outsiders which is included into the idea project.

A few years ago, the Swiss Railways (SBB) recognised the need to address young target groups more effectively and considered what would interest and excite young people. The marketing people had lengthy discussions and came up with a solution: special weekend offers for teenagers with train compartments which have been transformed into discos. SBB came to BrainStore with this idea. They asked us to test the idea on some young people to make sure that it really was good. The young people listened to the idea – and found it boring. "The train service's strength is trains not discos" was the general message in the feedback. SBB asked us to rethink the idea together with young people, experts and specialists. The result was "Track 7", a railcard for young people up to the age of 26, which on payment of a one-off charge per year enables them to travel free on all trains in Switzerland from 7 p.m. until the last train at night. The cooperation between insiders (customers) and outsiders (young people/experts) led to a much more interesting idea than the attempt by the SBB marketing experts.

What is a good idea?

A really good idea is simple, unexpected and relevant. And it unites extremes: it should risk a lot but nevertheless be easy to implement. Everyone should talk about it, but existing customers should not be irritated by it. It needs to be scientifically and academically flawless and nevertheless highly innovative. Or you would like to create a new service which the customers regard as revolutionary, but is still supportable for the employees. Perhaps you would like to considerably simplify procedures without annoying those concerned. Or give a product design a facelift without losing existing customers.

If you're looking for an idea, then you need to consider all the "ifs" and "buts" right from the start. You're always looking for the "as well as". The attractiveness of the idea can't be allowed to suffer through this. It still needs to be simple, unexpected and relevant.

> A good idea is simple, unexpected and relevant

A good mix leads to the best result

Creating such ideas is a balancing act, something which, at first sight, is impossible to achieve, almost like uniting two different cultures. In short: a feat of strength. A lot of people who are looking for ideas fail this feat of strength because they make a decisive mistake: they try to create an extreme without thinking in extremes. They leave the generation of ideas to a homogenous group, usually people from within the company or an agency or consultants. A homogenous group of people has a homogenous view of things. It stays within a framework, doesn't examine extremes, doesn't ask unexpected questions, doesn't doubt facts, dogmas and unwritten laws. A group of people who all think in the same way may get on very well, but they will only create monotonous ideas. Ursula Renold, the Deputy Director of the Swiss Federal Agency for Vocational Education and Technology, one of our clients, summed it up perfectly: "all of the ideas which we develop in our closed circle, are simply references to existing ideas". These referential ideas all move in one direction, are foreseeable, rarely rub up the wrong way and go with the flow of the corporate culture. Who's going to get enthusiastic about them? Who will they irritate? And who will defend such ideas and convince others until they suddenly also want to support the idea?

Important innovations rub people up the wrong way

Ideas which are generated by homogenous groups are usually not important innovations. It is uncomfortable to generate and carry through important innovations and it takes a lot of work. The implementation of a good idea is also not simply part of daily business and is therefore considered to be complicated and is not treated as a priority.

An example from DuPont shows this clearly: DuPont, one of the world's leading manufacturers of synthetic materials (for example, Teflon and Lycra) had developed a biologically degradable polymer called BioMax. This material has extremely interesting characteristics; one of which is the fact that it decomposes on contact with water. The developers of this material, now faced the question of where it could be used or to whom it could be of interest. The search for ideas was difficult for a number of reasons: the scientists themselves were not in a position to describe their fantastic material in simple words. The colleagues who dealt with other materials and had already positioned them successfully on the market, were regarded more as competitors than as suppliers of ideas. And the management didn't see it as their task to help in the generation of ideas. The clouds on the horizon only started to disappear when BrainStore suggested bringing the scientists together with outsiders and developing ideas in a structured way. Instead of fiddling about with the question "what are we going to do with our material?", we asked the question "imagine you are a microbe. What would you like to eat?", for example. Extremely interesting possibilities for using BioMax came up immediately, thanks to the collision of three universes (customers/outsiders/the right question) in cigarette ends, for example, or in the sticks for ice-lollies.

It is only human that a homogenous group faced with a new idea which brings a lot of work and uncertainty with it in preparation and in the implementation phases, instinctively shrinks back and decides to go take the easy route. Complex projects and daring ideas are scary at first. People block, because they are scared of the risks, see technical challenges coming at them and have visions of the word "flop" drifting across the horizon like a fata morgana. The fear of creating a huge flop and thereby risking your career is one of the most common reasons that new ideas are not implemented or not even discovered. Additionally, thinking in compartments is strongly manifested: innovations are usually the responsibility of research and development and other areas do not dare to approach the subject or they shrink back from the difficulties involved.

For this reason, many of the products and services sold as innovations today are nothing more than a marginal development of and small improvements to existing products. There is nothing wrong with such improvements: they are very important for the life cycle of a product. But they should not really be sold as innovations.

A new product or a new service nowadays needs to be differentiated from its predecessors and from competitive products. You can, of course, differentiate at the levels of price and marketing, but only up to a certain point, as the playing field is much smaller here. Real differentiation only happens as a result of a new idea. And a new idea is only good if it brings a real differentiation to the existing with it. Homogenous groups only manage that very rarely.

Killer expressions mean the death of every idea

The second thing that is missing when a homogenous group starts looking for an idea is the playful, creative component in the idea generation process. If the inside view predominates in the search, then the search will not get up to speed however good it may methodically be. Instead of helping the search for ideas, the participants put the brakes on. Career considerations, possessiveness, hierarchical considerations and self-censor stand in the foreground, as shown in the famous "killer expressions"

- I already know that
- We've tried that before
- The competition already does that
- It's much too expensive
- We can't do that
- There are technical difficulties
- The boss will say no to that
- It doesn't fit our image
- We'll make ourselves look ridiculous
- We don't know enough about that
- That can't be implemented

People who say no to everything attack fresh ideas like sharks

They are real idea brakes, which make the process tough and unattractive. Do you really believe that really unexpected ideas can be found in a tough and unattractive process?

If it's always the same people who circle around an idea, then killer arguments are the first things which appear, and not new ideas. Every new idea is looked at through the "why that can't possibly work" glasses instead of the "how could that work?" glasses. This destroys idea treasures, before they can even be lifted up.

In addition to those who say "No", there are also those who say "Mine": nowadays, most people believe that ideas belong to someone It is considered to be advantageous for your career development to have a good idea and bring it into play at the right time. A good idea therefore, should primarily serve the individual's objectives and only after that benefit the company or even the market. If I tell people about my idea at the wrong time, or tell the wrong person, then that could have a negative effect on my career. The idea could be rejected or, a few weeks later be propagated by the "wrong person". That's the end of my promotion, and my motivation. This can even block the exchange between the various groups in a company. In response to the question concerning product innovations brought out by the other worldwide groups of Nestlé in a certain year a high-ranking manager said to us "we don't even want to know, otherwise they'll come to us and steal our innovations" I still haven't understood what's supposed to be bad about exchanging product innovations throughout the world within the same company.

"That was my idea!" or "you stole my idea" is what you then hear in this climate of possessiveness. The strange thing is that people are usually pleased to talk about their ideas, and they actually enjoy sharing their thoughts with other people. It is a corporate culture which makes people possessive with their ideas, by rewarding them for this behaviour. Only then does someone feel the need to own "his" idea and keeps it to himself for as long as possible, to use it for his own benefit at some point instead of telling it to other people and sharing it with them, in order that everyone can benefit from it.

We take a completely different approach at BrainStore. We are convinced that an idea gets better, the more and the more diverse the people who are allowed to work on it. The process pulls together many pieces of a jigsaw and makes them into a good idea; this is then simply the logical final product of a well-managed process, in the same way that chocolate is the final product in a clearly defined sequence of working steps in a chocolate factory. We are well aware that there is also inspiration and a creative spirit in the process of manufacturing chocolate. It's no different in the generation of ideas: of course we need inspiration, chaos, curiosity and unorthodox thinkers, yet these are part of the process and not individual performances. This is one of the reasons why BrainStore remunerates everyone who takes part in an idea generation process with a predetermined payment. Everyone who contributes something, even if it is only a question or a smile at the right moment in time, has contributed something to the success of the idea. An idea generation process needs people who motivate and drive others, people who observe and people who analyse. Different perspectives and different skills contribute much more to a good idea than a single person however brilliant he may be.

History does, of course, provide any number of examples of brilliant flashes of inspiration from individual people, zany inventors and "crazy" engineers. And this method of idea generation has its validity alongside the systematic search for ideas. But is a mad scientist just as likely to guarantee a suggestion which is accepted and can be implemented as our heterogeneous group?

Letting worlds collide

If you take this principle of mixing insiders and outsiders in your CreatingCommunity to heart in your search for ideas, you've already gained a lot. At BrainStore, we have perfected the inclusion of external perspectives. In the first phase of idea generation, the collection of inspiration, we mix the insiders from the company, i.e. our client and their employees, with absolute outsiders and thus let completely different worlds collide from the very beginning. The ideal outsiders for our process are young people between 14 and 20 years of age, either from Switzerland or from the most varied countries of the world, depending on the project. What sounds very risky and adventurous at first sight, has been a tried and tested procedure for fourteen years at BrainStore, which benefits all participants in the idea generation process. The mix of teenagers and decision makers has a number of positive effects, which have a direct effect on the above-mentioned idea killers:

- Young people are refreshingly cheeky and unaffected. This acts like a highly contagious virus in a joint workshop with decision-makers.
- Teenagers are honest and direct. They say what they think and as a result often also have a disarming effect. Take 13-year old Daniel from London for example, he once asked the assembled top management of the fashion store C&A if they themselves wore clothes from C&A. One after the other they admitted through gritted teeth, that, at most, their socks and underwear came from C&A. Daniel thought about it for a few seconds and then said: "And so why do you expect us to wear the clothes?" Everyone laughed and then, visibly relieved, got back to work, namely looking for fresh ideas for C&A.
- Young people can work quickly and efficiently and, through this, push the managers included in the process to top performance. In many of our projects, our customers are amazed how the teenagers are still boiling over with ideas and carry on fantasising at the end of a day's work. This "work ethic" is contagious and transfers the impression that work can be fun.
- Hierarchies in a team become a non-subject through the inclusion of young people: because young people are not interested in hierarchies and because they set to work so spontaneously that the executives usually start to do the same thing sooner or later. We have had examples of management teams who had addressed each other formally using surnames for years and who suddenly started to call each other by their first names during the course of the idea generation process. And I have seen managers really thaw in the presence of the teenagers and tell us after the workshop that they felt as though they had been in a fountain of youth. By the way, we tell the young people before we start work, that the managers almost certainly are more afraid of them than they are of the managers; and that really is true. Many experienced managers have called us the day before an idea generation workshop to ask what they should wear and how they should behave.

- Young people work efficiently and quickly and find it easy to concentrate. They show our clients that work provides good results and can nevertheless be combined with a lot of fun. Our clients are regularly amazed how long teenagers can concentrate on a task, how quickly they pick things up and how much fresher they are at the end of an eight-hour workshop than the managers who are used to stress.
- Teenagers really do pick things up very quickly and haven't yet lost their childlike curiosity completely despite several years in the school system. They take up information quickly and link it cleverly with other information and knowledge. In some cases, the young people really do know nothing about a product or a service at the beginning of a workshop; they only learn roughly what it's about in the "info centre", a short programme block in which the client or BrainStore briefly presents the subject matter of the idea search. I have listened to the questions of young people on all manner of subjects from the disposal of nuclear waste, the way in which selected herbicides work or the functioning of a luxury business jet to typical youth topics such as event marketing, drinks, home entertainment or music, and I really have to correct every pessimist who complains about the lack of interest of today's youth. Young people often ask the decisive questions due to their honesty and natural naivety.
- Young people are not possessive with regard to ideas. They have fun playing with new solutions, building castles in the sky, creating crazy suggestions. A young participant in our Creative-Teams will never ask himself if what he is doing makes sense or not. He just dives head first into the water and feels like a fish immediately. Young people enjoy other people's ideas and develop them further, by finding a new version, taking an extreme perspective or asking a lot of questions. By doing so, they provide our clients with new trains of thought. Many of our clients suddenly say "I never thought of it like that" and are prepared for the first time to look at a subject in a different way.
- Killer expressions such as "won't work", "already tried it", "already know it", "completely stupid" are foreign to young people, because they are not embedded in company structures. They look at new suggestions with curiosity and are happy to develop them further

instead of immediately killing them with a compelling argument. A teenager is therefore capable of making a hardnosed aircraft engineer waste a few minutes' thoughts on what would happen if the cockpit in a plane was moved from the very front to the very back and attractive viewing points were added at the front (a suggestion the engineer would never have voiced himself and ultimately ended up as a completely different idea: providing the passengers with the view from the cockpit by having a camera transfer the angle of vision of the pilots to the screens in the seats).
- And, young people represent a new generation which feels at ease with new technologies, marketing techniques, advertising and PR as no generation before them.

Since 1989, I've been watching how young people and decision-makers start working together on something within minutes, how they create something new together without criticising the existing, how they had fun and laughed together. I have seen how people who otherwise would never have exchanged a word with each other, trod new paths together under enormous time pressure. I have seen how two totally different groups meet each other with respect, curiosity and inventiveness. These meetings fill me with pleasure every day of my working life and with respect for the insiders and outsiders who risk this step.

Even highly sceptical people, who initially faced the process with a lack of trust pick up speed to such an extent after a rather sluggish warm-up phase that they can hardly be stopped. Imagine a 13-year old schoolboy sitting on the floor with the marketing manager of a bank and they are both completely lost in a subject, drawing on a poster.

How does the network work?

You will have difficulties in building up a systematic network of outsiders yourself or in using teenagers in your internal idea generation projects. When designing "your" group, however, it will help you if you understand why and how we at BrainStore do it, how our network functions and how we select the workshop participants.

All the teenagers who take part in our network are registered in a database with their individual skills. A skill, for example, can be the ability to speak another language, particularly good Internet skills, a childhood in an exotic country or a hobby such as being the editor of a school magazine or leading a boy scouts group. Depending on the project, a group is then put together with the important skills for the project concerned. We publish the participation in a project as a job opportunity in the Internet or in other channels. The potential participants apply for the job and provide information on their skills (in many cases they have to prove certain skills using a questionnaire) and we are then in the fortunate position of being able to invite the most suitable people to the project. This all works web-based using an application on any commercially available large database. The members of the network can continuously expand and update their data and skills. Just a trip to Burma can, for example, assist in gaining the new skill "exotic traveller" or "Asia expert", if the member of the CreatingCommunity can show in an appropriate way what he or she learned and experienced on the trip. The teams for the work are carefully mixed from people with different interests, from different regions, age groups and different levels of education. We thus create a very heterogeneous team.

Young people who have already taken part in various projects can take advantage of advancement possibilities and train as moderators, minute-takers or project managers. They therefore remain in the network even when they have left their youth behind them and are often included as experts in their professional area. A good example of such a career is Laurent, our 24-year old communications manager. His BrainStore career started when he was 12 years old and he took part in an idea project for the first time. We already noticed in the first project that Laurent is very clever. Laurent cleverly links all the facts and information from the project with his very broadly based general knowledge and bursts with good ideas. At that time Laurent was a rather hyperactive pubescent child with too much energy, but fortunately with parents who knew how to actively stretch their child's ability. In addition to cello and piano lessons, his own school magazine project and various artistic projects, BrainStore offered him a platform to deal with this energy, and Laurent has never disappointed us in all the years. Apart from participating in idea workshops, he regularly worked on internal projects in the holidays. Because he was so young he stayed overnight with BrainStore employees. They always received telephone calls from Laurent's mum in the evening to check whether her youngster really had cleaned his teeth properly. That was the least of our worries, it was difficult enough trying to find his "off" switch towards midnight and persuade him to think about going to bed. He was project leader for the first time at 16 for a project to create a magazine on the subject of nutrition for a target group of 14 to 18-year olds. It was a very hot summer and I will never forget pushing Laurent fully-clothed into the 24 degree warm Biel lake to make him finally inwardly and outwardly cool down as he was hyperventilating after an never-ending discussion on the potential name of the magazine. Today, Laurent lives in Berlin and in Biel, a week here and a week there and looks after all BrainStore's communication projects, from mailings and brochures to PR and new contacts. There are numerous employees like Laurent, who are loosely connected to BrainStore and can become active again in projects for our clients.

A small network spreads

BrainStore started in 1989 with a very modest network of teenagers from Switzerland. We invited them to projects with clients who wanted to get to know the target group "youth" better – and who dared to sit down at a table with them. In the late eighties, the opinion was prevalent in Switzerland, that "young people" are people between the ages of five and twenty-five who can be won over for any product on earth with an advertising claim in English, chart music and loud colours. What a big mistake. Anyone who looked at the target group youth more closely even then, found out that "the youth" is divided into diverse subcultures and that young people – just like adults – are not all interested in the same thing, but in a wide variety of different subjects.

One of our first projects was to develop a presence for the STOP-AIDS campaign of the Swiss Ministry of Health, which would be compatible with the interests of 15 to 19-year olds. For this purpose, teenagers from all over Switzerland came to the then advertising agency of the STOP-AIDS campaign in Bern and developed and evaluated various ideas, one of which was particularly convincing: a double-page ad was placed in magazines for school kids. A piece of chewing gum was glued in on the left, sponsored by Hollywood chewing gum, and underneath the words "for kissing". On the right side, a condom was glued, in a pack decorated with a red heart with the footnote "against Aids". The ad was a hit in schools in Switzerland. At that point in time, the subject of Aids was still taboo, and many schools, particularly the catholic boarding schools, were enraged by the ad. The trick was that the ad was publicised through the school magazines which are independent of the school management in Switzerland both financially and with regard to content, the only step they could take was to prohibit the sale of the magazine on school grounds, which, of course, dramatically increased sales directly in front of the school gates.

We gradually included teenagers in all kinds of idea generation projects: those which concerned the target group youth, but also others in which we, for example, had to look at the typical BMW driver. Our methodology of systematically including young people has proved itself in every project over the fourteen years.

Experts, Specialists and Lateral Thinkers

In our network of freelancers, which now spans the whole world, you won't only find young people, but also experts, specialists and thinkers of every kind: from professors at various universities, a chocolate specialist, a nutrition adviser, a breathing therapist, a circus director or a specialist for amphibians in the wild to a smokejumper (he jumps out of an airplane into a fire, with the intention of extinguishing it). We have an "explanation designer" in the network, who can do nothing else (so he says himself) but explain things which are difficult for people to understand in simple figurative language. We also have a female vicar, who used to be a male vicar, a film producer, a robotics expert, a wildlife specialist, an opera singer, product designer, graphic designers, technical people, developers, nursery nurses, teachers, psychologists, a japanologist, political scientists and many, many more. They come from Switzerland, Germany, Austria, England and France, from the USA, the Netherlands, Mexico, India, Japan, Singapore, Hong Kong, Brazil, China and other corners of the world. The network is growing every day (the current status is around 2,500 members, of which around half are young people). Our network doesn't work on the basis of fixed cooperation, but as a loose connection, which is activated when a project requires those specialist skills. The specialists apply for jobs in just the same way as the teenagers, by listing their skills, which are tested if necessary.

When someone is included in a project, then they play a part for a clearly defined duration of time and then leave the project. Depending on the function, a commitment can last for a few hours (for participants in an ideas workshop, for example), a few days (for trend scouts or for IdeaInterviews, for example) or for several months (for a project manager, for example). What is important is that it is always only an obligation towards the current project in each case. The system of inviting people to apply guarantees us that we can include those persons in the project who are relevant for the project at that time, have enough time available and are motivated to work hard on the project.

The system can be adjusted continuously and functions according to the principle of optimisation: if we only have restricted time available for the search for ideas, then we look for participants and project members in the close vicinity of our offices and, where necessary due to time considerations, make compromises in the selection because the most important thing in the project is speed. Our client nevertheless gets a mixed team which corresponds to our principle of including insiders and outsiders. If we have more time and a higher budget, then we can widen our search for suitable project freelancers from our CreatingCommunity and put together a really optimally mixed team, often including high-level experts.

BrainStore assembles a completely new team of freelancers for every project. This avoids preconceived ideas, hierarchical thinking and burnout. The effort needed to lead such a team is considerable and the coaching of the individual functions needs to be very well conceived. What we get out of it is, in addition to a perfect mix, high flexibility and efficiency.

Sensitive Projects

Many of our clients are concerned about confidentiality and security when they first hear about this network. The fact is that we have never had a problem with that in all the fourteen years we have been in business. The first reason is that all project participants who come from outside the company never have all information on the project available to them, only the points which are relevant for them. More importantly however, is that our relaxed attitude towards the idea of "security" has certainly contributed to the fact that our participants don't even think about "confidentiality". They just work with us on a new idea, are usually also told who the client is (unless this is expressly not wanted) and, once the project has been successfully completed, are also informed of the results by us. Because we do not reward individual performance, but the work in a clearly defined project, we also have never had a problem with possessiveness of ideas. Everyone who works with us is fully aware that he contributes a piece of the jigsaw to the success of the whole project.

It is also important to assemble a completely new team for each project so that burnout syndrome never even happens.

We do of course take our clients' desire for discretion and the protection of sensitive data seriously. Every participant in a project signs an agreement that the data and information in the project may only be used as part of the project. We consider any further warning or reference to be superfluous or even contra productive.

Insiders and outsiders in company innovation

So what can you do to develop ideas as a company innovator which are simple, unexpected and at the same time, relevant? You can include extreme positions in every innovation project right from the beginning. The three most relevant are the internal and external perspective and a neutral process management. People who work in your company automatically support an internal perspective. People who work outside the company automatically support an external perspective. Only mixing the two groups will allow the development of unexpected and new ideas. Neutral process management enables a structured procedure.

Simply including different hierarchy levels and representatives of different functional areas in the company will enable you to significantly widen the perspective from which the idea is viewed and therefore gain a lot. Have you thought of including the woman who serves the meals in your canteen in a idea generation process? You can be sure that she would have a few things to contribute.

But perspectives from within the company won't be enough to come up with really simple, unexpected and relevant ideas. You should also include people from the outside. You probably won't succeed in getting any teenagers to the table, but you could try it with students. Avoid those who have already developed into people who have no other interests outside their own subject. Trainees in your company could also be a good option, as they come close to teenagers with their external perspective, but are nevertheless available within the company. You must, of course, manage and control a workshop with insiders and outsiders very closely.

Think, both with insiders and outsiders, about which perspectives you actually want. Experienced experts are often much less interesting than users. When we developed new ideas for medicine packaging for DuPont, for example, we didn't include packaging experts, but several members of the nursing staff of a nearby hospital. Their expert knowledge from the daily usage of the packaging was more valuable for us in this stage than the opinion of highly qualified packaging designers who presumably had little contact with the real world. Consider which perspective you need most urgently for your project. Is it the user's perspective? Or the perspective of an expert rooted in theory? Do you perhaps also need a lateral thinker, who questions everything and looks at everything in a completely different way to you? We can only advise you not to surround yourself with comfortable people, who always do what you ask them, but with uncomfortable people who question what you do from morn to night and sometimes drive you to despair. This will be of much more use to your idea generation project and bring you much further.

In addition to the composition of the team, neutral process management is very important. When it comes to ideas, everyone wants to have their say, and that's OK. But having your say and playing a role in decisions needs to be guided and independently controlled. You also need someone from time to time, who guides the project with a certain amount of authority.

Example of a balanced team for a demanding idea generation project

Internal perspective
- The engineer from the development department with his subject-specific knowledge
- The managing director with his authority
- The production line supervisor who has perfect knowledge of the machines
- The marketing manager because she is responsible for the idea
- The curious trainee in the marketing department
- Representatives of sales and finance

External perspective
- Eight students (both male and female)
- An expert on Russia (because the project concerns the Russian market)
- Your three best customers

Who should manage it?
- An experienced facilitator. He can even stand up to the engineer who always says "No".

Core Concepts "CreatingCommunity"

- Include both insiders and outsiders in every idea generation project and ensure that there is neutral, competent management.
- Search for as many different perspectives as possible within the company and from outside of it. Ideal participants are, for example, students, housewives, young people and people within the company who are not usually involved in idea generation projects. You can also use specialists, customers or consultants as experts and specialists.
- The size of the group for an idea workshop should be between eight people as a minimum and maximum 200 people; ideally there is a balanced relationship between insiders and outsiders. In later stages of the project, smaller groups will be sufficient, which are mostly made up of experts (four to six people including the project management).
- Pay the participants well for their efforts and ensure that copyrights are covered by this fee. Define the amount of work exactly for the participants. What is expected from them, what will be the duration of their participation, which preconditions do they need to meet? Make agreements in advance concerning confidentiality, copyrights and the desired input (specialist area, perspective).
- Your participants should be expressly invited as team players; individualists, or people who want to stand out from the crowd at any price, disrupt the process. Stress that you are looking for new input and perspectives, but that the idea will be found in a joint process.
- Reward the participation in the process, the efforts to find a solution – and not personal idea results.
- In longer projects, have an outsider regularly review and criticise the ideas. Form a new team for each project step (the core team can, of course, remain in charge throughout the whole project).
- "Dare to share": be generous with project information to the participants. Don't hold on to information out of fear that something could leak out t the outside. Holding on to information won't bring up any new ideas. But make agreements with the participants on secrecy and confidentiality.

CreativeTeam

*Insiders and outsiders
collect raw ideas together*

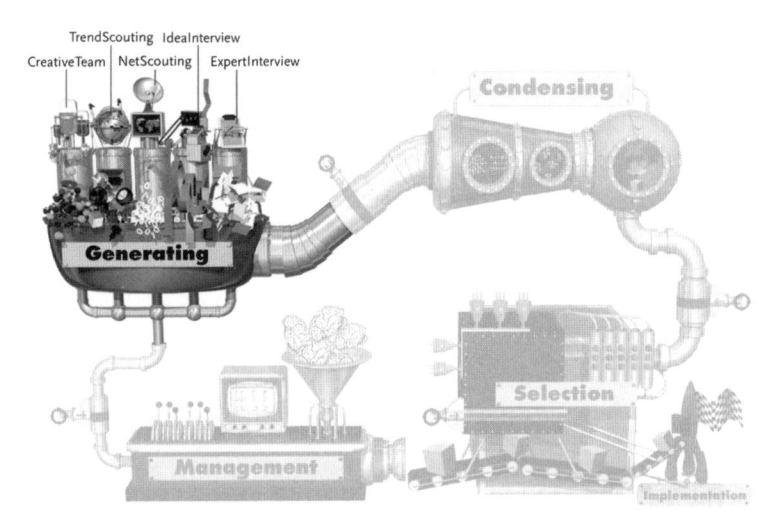

The CreativeTeam is the most important tool in the generation of raw material for your idea. In a workshop lasting between one and eight hours, insiders and outsiders together collect as many components for the idea as possible.

The composer Anton Bruckner once said "if you want to build high towers, you need to spend a long time working on the foundation". That doesn't only apply to music and every form of art, but also to ideas. If you want to produce good ideas, then the first phase of the project should be concerned with generating as many different seeds of ideas as possible. That is the foundation, the base work, which is necessary to achieve a really good result.

In the chapter "Briefing & KickOff", I sketched out how you can formulate a clear briefing and how you can divide this briefing into its component parts. In the chapter "CreatingCommunity", I advocated having insiders and outsiders work together on ideas, in order that something really new results. And in the chapter "A machine produces ideas", you learned that the various phases of the idea generation process (generating – condensing – decision – management) must be clearly separated from each other. These three principles – briefing, insider/outsider and separate phases – now take effect.

You really do need a CreativeTeam when looking for ideas: the CreativeTeam is a workshop, in which insiders and outsiders come together under professional guidance to generate ideas based on the briefing. No, actually they're not yet looking for complete ideas, just for idea particles, components, pieces, incomplete thoughts and notions. The objective is to illuminate a question from many different perspectives and to generate as many seeds and raw ideas as possible. It only very rarely happens that an implementable idea falls from heaven in the CreativeTeam – that's not what's wanted either. What does come up are even more crazy ideas and thoughts which serve as inspiration in the condensing phase of the project to be further developed and combined.

Bringing the right people to the right place

The minimum requirements for a CreativeTeam are 15 participants (a mix of insiders and outsiders), a capable and motivating facilitator, perhaps also a co-facilitator and at least one other person who takes down the results.

In addition, you need a large room with natural daylight. As a rule of thumb: the room should be capable of holding at least four times the number of actual participants who you have invited to the workshop. It makes sense to choose a room for the workshop which has as little as possible to do with your daily business. At BrainStore, the participants come into a crazy factory atmosphere with brightly-coloured walls, a carpet of artificial grass, industrial goods which have been transformed into furniture, weird decoration and several bathtubs. They are confronted with a completely strange atmosphere the minute they arrive, when they receive their name badge and working materials in an inflatable plastic bag in our pink "check-in" with airport departure boards.

The tool bag contains all the working materials which a CreativeTeam needs: writing pad and clipboard, scissors, glue, something to eat and drink and a small information brochure.

Of course we have fun in thinking up crazy interior decoration and adding new effects, but the decisive factor is the effect we create with our clients: we take them out of their daily office life the minute they walk into the unusual atmosphere of our premises. That clears their head. And in this phase we want clear heads.

You obviously can't copy such an atmosphere 1:1, but you can look for a similar atmosphere. And you obviously can't design your workshop room in such an extreme way as we do, because you presumably want to use it for another purpose afterwards ..., but you can still apply the principle.

When BrainStore produces ideas somewhere else, which happens quite frequently, then we do exactly the same thing: we look for a room which can trigger the same effect as ours: we're looking for a basic atmosphere which is distinctively different to the usual office environment and puts the participants into a positive and open frame of mind. We spend a lot of time and energy looking for such a room, because we know that the quality of the results depends heavily on whether the participants can really let go of their daily grind. That's what our experience has shown anyway: don't underestimate the effect of the environment. In your normal conference room, you will find well-worn paths, but no new roads.

Very good rooms are, for example, artists ateliers, photographers' lofts, factory halls, theatres, cinemas or sports halls. Sometimes a location which at first sight looks completely unsuitable is exactly the right thing. For a project for our client Syngenta for example, we needed to find a workshop room in Chicago. We knew that we were dealing with a rather conservative client and therefore did the rounds of all the more classic possibilities such as seminar centres and conference rooms. We weren't happy with any of the solutions, everything was too sterile and normal. Then we found a youth centre at the northern edge of the city of Chicago. The youth centre was used for all kinds of events such as "open microphone nights" or hip-hop concerts and had the corresponding alternative groove. There were, for example, 50 different chairs in the room; no two were alike. There were lots of useless but entertaining pieces of furniture and decorations lying around. The workshop room had a fantastic upper light and access to the backyard was also available; from there it was only around 200 meters to Lake Michigan, the huge lake which borders on Chicago. Natural daylight and access to the outside are ideal for the production of ideas: we immediately felt comfortable in this room. But would our client feel the same way? We decided to take the risk. After thoroughly cleaning the place, temporarily removing 80 percent of the furniture and using an air freshener, which efficiently covered a lingering smell of hemp, the room was perfect for our purposes. And what happened? Both the client and the outsiders felt comfortable in the atmosphere and could produce fantastic ideas together.

A criticism-free attitude

The quality of the results depends decisively on designing a CreativeTeam which will be free of criticism and open for new things. The sole purpose of the workshop is to gather material, which automatically also results in waste being generated. In fact, most of it is waste; that has to happen. But, at first you never know what is going to be waste and what will later turn out to be a gold nugget. Look upon the generation of raw ideas as an adventure, in which you sometimes carry a stone down from the mountain on the assumption that it contains a crystal – you drag the stone with you based only on this assumption and you are prepared to wait to see if the stone really will surprise you with valuable contents.

In the same way, a seemingly valueless idea can turn into a precious stone when you are looking for ideas. The Brazilian aircraft company Embraer wanted to find out how the regional jet could develop in terms of interior design, entertainment, seat alignment and communication in the future. In the CreativeTeam in which aircraft engineers, marketing specialists, pilots and young people took part, we asked, amongst other things, the following question. "How does an airplane need to be fitted out and designed, so that the passengers never want to get off?" Eight groups worked on this task for ten minutes each using a paper plane and handicraft materials. The objective was to build and label a model and present it to the other groups.

Thanks to the participation of the young people in each group, the work was highly dynamic so that each group actually could present an interesting model at the end of the ten minutes. It was amazing: five of the eight groups had built a swimming pool into the plane and four had considered moving the cockpit from the front to the back to provide viewing places at the front. Both approaches would certainly never have come up in a classic brainstorming session with engineers, as they cannot be implemented. In our CreativeTeam however, they were permitted and even desired. These unusual and unrealistic ideas are necessary in order to create something realistic and unexpected in the next phase of the project.

In the case of the Embraer project, the swimming pools became refresher sprays in every seat and the viewing points became cameras in various places in the plane with which every passenger received unusual and interesting views delivered to his seat via monitor. Five years later, this technology is now used in many airplanes.

Good question

The questions in the CreativeTeam should be as simple and uncomplicated as possible: A few examples:

- *"How would Madonna promote herself if she wanted to become President of the United States?"* (a Swiss political party, "last minute election campaign ideas" project)
- *"Develop a cap for a drink which can be opened in the dark!"* (SIG Combibloc, "ideas for new caps" project)
- *"What would a person from Mars call this product?"* (Migros retail stores, "new drink for young people" project)
- *"If you were a microbe, what would you like to eat?"* (DuPont, "ideas for applications for the biologically degradable synthetic material BioMax" project)
- *"Write down 50 words which all begin with the letters LUM!"* (Syngenta, "finding a name for a new herbicide" project)
- *If you were the Head of C&A, what would you change in the stores?"* (C&A, "making the sales floors interesting for young people" project)

Only when the question is put so simply that a teenager can understand it without having to ask twice, can we assume that interesting idea fragments will result. Preparing such questions is, therefore, a precondition for good ideas and belongs to the preparation of such a workshop. It is particularly important that the questions do not include any foreign words, intellectual formulations or facts which are difficult to comprehend. A single question is usually not enough to receive enough interesting basic ideas. At least six questions are necessary for a one-hour workshop and maximum 30 questions for a six-hour workshop in order to achieve good results.

You can find out if the question formulation is good in a short test-run which you can carry out with your moderator and a few voluntary test participants on the day before the CreativeTeam. You will notice very quickly whether the questions flow smoothly and convincingly from the moderator to the participants and whether the participants can develop unexpected ideas. If the moderator stumbles when he formulates the question or if he has to start explaining things, then you need to rework the question. And if the participants only produce boring output, then you make need to think about the technique you are working with. Experience shows however, that you can come up with interesting and useable material with a simple question formulation and a suitable technique. Wait a minute: technique? What is meant by technique?

Use a variety of techniques

You don't only need simple questions, but also techniques with which the questions are linked. It is impossible to expect the participants in a workshop to patiently sit Hat a table for two hours and cheerfully produce ideas. Techniques are varied activities, which are linked with the question formulation for the idea search and which activate different parts of the brain (sometime creative skills are needed, sometimes linguistic skills, sometimes the ability to visualise three-dimensionally and sometimes abstract skills). They guarantee that all participants – for six hours if necessary – can concentrate and are motivated on the subject.

At BrainStore, we use over 100 different tools and keep creating new techniques, which are tailored to the clients' questions. Those clients in particular, who have already worked with us on several projects, want to be surprised by new activities all the time. If you need some good techniques for your idea generation project, then you can copy our most important "classics". These have been tried and tested thousands of times and can be used by you in a simple manner.

Brainstorming

Classic brainstorming, which you probably know well, is a meaningful and good technique – but only when it is carried out creatively. A brainstorming session according to the principles of industrial idea production lasts between 5 and 15 minutes and can answer a question with many variations. For example: which functions could chocolate have specifically for children, young people, senior citizens, managers, Mars men? For the brainstorming session you will need a moderator, someone who can quickly take down what is said (two would be better), and a flipchart or a video-beamer, which is connected to the PC of the person making the notes.

Rules for brainstorming:

- Everyone can say everything which occurs to them (even if it sound stupid or meaningless at first sight).
- Everything is allowed, except criticism. People who constantly criticise or make comments ("we've already said that!"), can be excluded from the brainstorming session using the red card.
- If something has not been written down, repeat it until it is written down.
- If something occurs to you which has already been said, say it again.
- Speak loudly and clearly.

The facilitator asks the first question and lets the brainstorming session go on for as long as required until it starts to slow down. Then he asks the next question. He can make the brainstorming session more interesting by making the people move: having them stand up, stand on the chairs, change places, change the scene (for example, by leaving the room).

The quality of a brainstorming session depends very much on the quality of the moderator and on the speed of the person doing the writing; if it goes too slowly, a brainstorming session can quickly become boring; if it is well moderated and dynamic, it makes a lot of fun and does bring really unexpected results.

The rule "say everything which occurs to you" is particularly important for good brainstorming. In our CreativeTeams, we always tell our participants as an example, that they should say everything, even if it's only "strawberry yoghurt". And you can be sure of one thing: in almost every brainstorming session, whether it's about space travel or office furniture, you hear the word "strawberry yoghurt" at least once. Brainstorming is suitable for questions in which the participants can provide each other with inspiration, for example, for very visionary ideas or for associations. In a five-minute brainstorming session with 15 participants, around 250 inspirations can be collected – 50 per minute: that means high speed! A brainstorming session like that should not last longer than 15 minutes.

BrainWriting

In BrainWriting, the participants write their ideas on pre-prepared forms. Always one idea per sheet.

The technique of BrainWriting is a good way of collecting sound, varied ideas. It is a technique which can be carried out by the participants individually or in groups.

To prepare it, the question formulation must be coupled with an appropriate worksheet. If, for example, the question is "How do you make it clear to the purchasers of this product, that it is now even better?", then an appropriate worksheet would have a picture of the product and, beside it, an empty star shape to be written in.

All participants receive a pile of these worksheets and start to fill them out. It is important that a new sheet is used for each idea and that the participants waste no time thinking about what they have written. The moderator should make sure that the participants just keep filling out one sheet after the other. A good average duration for a BrainWriting session is three minutes per question. The sheets are then simply placed on the floor or in a box and then collected and minuted by the minute-taker. With 15 participants, this results in at least 400 inspirations.

BrainStation

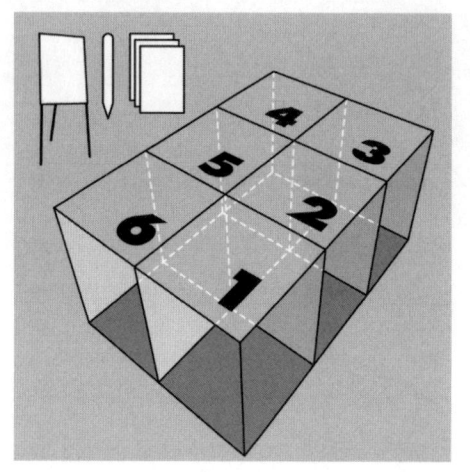

In the Brainstation, the participants travel through six stations and note their ideas to a specific question at each station for three minutes while inspiring music is played.

The BrainStation is a good way of looking at a question from different perspectives in a very short period of time. For a BrainStation, you need six isolated group work stations. At BrainStore, these are six separate working boxes which each hold eight people, our "Mini Labs" and when we are travelling, we use six mobile tents. The important thing is that the participants can work in parallel at six different points without disturbing each other. Number the stations to make it easier to navigate between them. You need six questions for a BrainStation exercise, for which you want to collect ideas. Print the questions on large sheets and pin them at eyelevel at each station so that the participants can see at a glance what it's about. You additionally need one or two flipcharts with enough paper and writing material (wide pens or refillable board markers are best) at each station.

If you like, you can also illustrate or decorate the stations appropriately to the question, so that it acts as inspiration for the participants. When we were looking for ideas for a name change for a chain of restaurants for example, we decorated each of the six stations like different restaurants, with set tables, pictures and decoration elements from typically Swiss through Asian to Mexican. The objective of this exercise was to develop as many exotic sounding names as possible. Or you could simply support the question with a suitable picture. If you like music as work support and find it inspiring, then find suitable music for the exercise and prepare six sequences of one minute each.

The participants are divided into six groups by the moderator and distributed over the stations. As soon as the music starts, the participants note ideas to the question on the flipcharts in their respective stations. Drawings or sketches are of course also allowed if the question permits them. After three minutes, the groups move to the next station, where the exercise immediately continues. After 20 minutes (18 minutes working time and 2 minutes travelling time between stations), you have collected around 800 inspirations with 15 participants. The BrainStation is suitable for every type of question, which can be looked at from various perspectives and also for CreativeTeams in which you only have a short time to generate inspiration. This technique delivers a lot of inspirations in a very short period of time.

BrainRace

It's all about speed in the BrainRace: who can write down the most ideas in the shortest time?

BrainRace is my favourite technique because it corresponds most closely to our philosophy of the industrial search for ides. As opposed to school, where you are told to "think first, and then write", we operate on the "write first and then think" principle, and the thinking comes much, much later. We sometimes need to use a few tricks to make sure that our participants take this to heart. BrainRace is one of these tricks. This fast-paced technique for looking for ideas switches off the participants' brains and lets them work on the instinctive level only.

As the name says, BrainRace is a technique which involves a lot of running. You need a lot of room for it. If the weather is good, then you can hold a BrainRace outside, but it also works in a long corridor, in a factory or in a very large conference room. In addition to sufficient space, you also need masses of worksheets with room for ten ideas on each, writing materials and a clipboard and a green stamp.

The BrainRace takes place between two stations which are at least ten metres apart. At one station, the participants each write ten ideas one each worksheet. At the other station, the moderator (and two helpers if possible) waits for the onrush of the masses. The participants run to the moderator with their filled in worksheets, get an OK stamp for every legible idea and then run back to the first station where the next ten ideas are written down. The participants collect their worksheets with the help of a clipboard (available in specialist stores). The person who has collected the most green stamps at the end of the exercise is the winner. You will have organised the prize in advance – nothing big, a bar of chocolate, a magazine, an amusing game.

BrainRace is fun and is very productive. Even otherwise rather shy participants, who are unsure if they will be able to produce ideas, become real champions in this exercise. I have experienced groups, who approached the exercise in a very sporting manner and were completely out of breath in ten minutes. For safety reasons, you should always ensure that the path between station one and station two is completely clear of obstacles and that the participants are made aware not to overdo it and not to injure themselves. We have carried out at least 500 BrainRaces since starting to use this technique, and no-one has yet been injured.

In a five-minute BrainRace with 15 participants, you can collect around 400 inspirations. And these inspirations come directly "from the stomach" of the participants, meaning that they haven't been rationally filtered or interpreted, which makes them particularly interesting. Interestingly, people who are sceptical or who always say "No" are often the most ambitious with this technique and are impressed by what they have achieved afterwards. I often experience that people who look grim or appear disinterested in the other workshops come out of themselves in this exercise and then usually have a smile on their face for the rest of the workshop. You see, stress can also make you happy.

BrainShaping

For BrainShaping, the participants need plastic modelling material, a knife for the precision work and labelling material to present ideas three dimensionally.

This technique works at the manual level and turns the participants into handicraft enthusiasts. It is particularly good for collecting pictorial and three dimensional ideas. We also often use it as an icebreaker. For this exercise it is best to have the participants work in groups of three. For each work group, you need plastic modelling material in six different colours (Play-doh, children's plastic modelling material works best), a piece of coated cardboard, Post-It notes, toothpicks and writing material. The task is to build a three dimensional model based on the question, make little flags with the toothpicks and the Post-It notes to label the models and then present the finished work to the other groups.

Everything is suitable as a question which can be answered pictorially or with an object, for example, *"Build an object which gets attention!"* or *"What will your dream restaurant look like in 50 years?"* or *"What kind of vehicle could be driven with this small motor?"*

The time budget for this task should be very short, in order that really amazing and unusual objects are developed and the groups have no time to talk themselves out of their courageous works of art and rebuild them. 15 to 20 minutes is ideal. It is very important that the objects are labelled. If this has been forgotten, then the person taking the notes during the presentation of the objects, must note exactly what is said in the oral presentation, so that no details are lost. The models should also be photographed, because they don't usually keep that long or they get broken. You must always ensure that the results can flow into the further process either as a picture or in the written form.

BrainShaping is highly suitable for getting started on a subject or to round off a subject in an artistic way. For complex subjects, we add further handicrafts materials to the plastic modelling material, which must be the same for each group. The materials should stimulate the imagination and not limit it. Plastic modelling material is usually enough, because you can make almost anything with it. It is important that the participants understand that they are not supposed to make beautiful objects, but that the idea behind the object counts.

I can remember a particularly impressive BrainShaping experience with the University of Geneva and the Business School IMD, who wanted to work with us on a project on the subject "Attention Management". The project concerned the question of how managers could increase the attention of their employees in important projects. In the CreativeTeam, we wanted to throw some light on various aspects around the subject of attention and find out how attention can be created. We had many top managers in the team, from Siemens, Deutsche Bank and Motorola amongst others. They were very sceptical about the inclusion of young people in this project and we knew that we needed to create an impressive experience right at the beginning of the project.

The first exercise was BrainShaping. Together with one of the young people, each manager created an object which created attention. After ten minutes, we had 45 objects in front of us, which impressively showed how many different ways there are to get attention and in how many different ways this is perceived. We had no further attention problems with our participants in the remaining workshop.

Using BrainShaping for ten to 20 minutes and with 15 participants, you can create between five and fifteen objects, which will give you an impression of what the finished idea could look like or what it could be about. It's also important that each group can briefly present its model to the other groups – that's good for motivation and the person taking the notes can note an exact description of the idea: there's also usually a lot to laugh about with most of the presentations.

In complex projects, BrainShaping can also be deigned completely freely. In a project for Nestlé, we had the task of developing new ideas for coffee-based drinks. We asked the client for an open budget to set up a drinks laboratory in which the CreativeTeam members could mix their own drinks. We rented five refrigerators, ten mixers, an ice machine, hotplates and bought a lorry load of all possible ingredients for a coffee drink, from milk and coffee to fruit, herbs, caramel sauce and spices, in total over 100 ingredients. In the BrainShaping session, the participants had half an hour to mix their drink combinations, give them names and present them to the other participants for tasting. The compositions were, in part, very adventurous and tasted that way too, for example the coffee-nutmeg-strawberry drink called "Commushake", but the notes on the results were an excellent inspiration for the rest of the work.

BrainCharting

In BrainCharting, the participants create a collage from current magazines on a certain subject or a clearly formulated question.

Working with pictures is often a good way of getting insiders and outsiders to work together. BrainCharting is a simple and visually stimulating technique, which most participants like doing. You need various newspapers and magazines, scissors, large posters and glue.

The technique is extremely suitable:

- for communicative questions, for example *"Create a poster, which will make millions of people like the new camembert cheese!"*
- for the search for arguments, for example *"Collect pictures and statements supporting the use of the new board computer in the BMW 7 series!"*
- for the search for picture worlds, for example *"In what kind of world would this chocolate be eaten?"*
- but also for abstract questions, such as *"Make a poster showing the ideal person for this job!"*.

BrainCharting is almost a meditative technique. Insiders and outsiders let themselves be inspired by magazines and first just cut out material on the question. They then almost intuitively start putting the pieces together to make a work of art which they label by explaining on the poster what they wanted to show. A BrainCharting session of around 15 minutes, with 15 participants divided into five groups will generate around 100 inspirations which can be used in the subsequent process.

The Programme

A CreativeTeam essentially consists of the following elements:
1. An icebreaker question, in which all participants introduce themselves and get to know each other a little better. This is necessary, because they are a mixed group of insiders and outsiders.
2. Various questions, derived from the idea briefing (see chapter "Briefing & KickOff"), the work technique most suitable for the question and, if required, the appropriate music.
3. An "information centre", in which the participants in the CreativeTeam learn a little more about the question in the idea search. We work on the principle "as little as possible, as much as necessary". The participants shouldn't be confused by long speeches and explanations, but should use their energy to find ideas. The fewer details they know about the project, the better. It is the task of the workshop leader to put the programme for the CreativeTeam together in such a way that they adopt the right perspective and collect the right seeds of ideas. The Information centre doesn't necessarily need to be at the beginning of the workshop, it can take place at a strategically advantageous point.
4. Regular, very short breaks with healthy and varied snacks. At BrainStore we serve fruit, popcorn, yoghurt or drinks.

Speed, speed, speed!

You have doubtless already visited a few workshops in seminars yourself. What I always notice is that you are given much too much time to come up with a result in these workshops. All dynamics are lost by this, because the people spend the first 20 minutes with small talk, then discuss the task half-heartedly, and then finally fill a flipchart with a few sentences just to have something which they can present.

If you want to create ideas, then you need to reverse this principle: provide too little time rather than too much. Every programme section at BrainStore is between ten and 20 minutes long. If you tell a group that they have to find a solution within ten minutes, then everyone will get a move on and be productive instead of thinking about possible problems, restrictions and technical obstacles. That doesn't mean that these things shouldn't be thought about at all, just that they should be thought about at the right time. And this right time comes later. When we're generating ideas, we don't want to know all the things which wouldn't work, but all the things which would be fantastic.

If you make limited time available, the adrenalin level of the participants increases. That does however, only work really well, if you mix outsiders and insiders. The teenagers we work with, take the amount of time given particularly seriously. If we say "You have three minutes time, start now!", then they really start then. It is usually the teenagers who spur our clients on to give their best. I once heard a 14-year old schoolboy say "What are you standing around for? We've got to work!" to two managers, and that's the way it happens in most CreativeTeams. Everyone gets to work pragmatically, efficiently and yet with a certain wink of the eye and set themselves the goal of astounding the other groups with their funny, crazy or completely unrealistic suggestions. And that – as I have often said already – is exactly what we are looking for.

Regardless of all ambition: it is never deadly serious in this group work. Most of the feedback questionnaires which our clients and the teenagers complete after the workshops, mention how much laughing went on. Laughter is also a measurement for us as to whether a programme works well or not. If there has been no hearty laughter after an hour, then something has gone wrong and we urgently need to adapt the programme.

Organisational issues

The participants can collect more inspired ideas if they feel at ease in the CreativeTeam. What happens in the background in such a workshop and how an atmosphere is created which the participants will remember for a long time is therefore of some significance. This includes the room, the catering, the tidying up, the quality of the working materials, the ventilation and, of course, the coffee! A large number of things which need to be thought about.

Your primary goal is, of course, to develop a good idea and you shouldn't let the background work develop into perfectionism. It is however, wise to take a few precautions. The most important two things are probably tidiness and the catering. Give one person, for example, one of your trainees, responsibility for ensuring that the working room and the break room are tidy during the workshop, meaning clearing away crockery, collecting material and putting it back where it belongs, cleaning tables, etc. You will be very grateful to this steward at the end of the workshop.

The catering issue is best outsourced, that saves time and nerves. Make sure there are enough healthy and tasty snacks available such as small sandwiches, popcorn, yoghurt, salt sticks or fruit. Avoid heavy food such as chocolate, sweet bars, potato crisps or generally fatty food: it will lay heavy in your participants' stomachs and divert their attention from the work.

The orchestration of the workshop, the procedure of the programme with breaks, highlights and technical details should be discussed in detail in advance by the workshop leadership team. In this way, you ensure that the participants give you the best possible compliment at the end of the workshop "We hardly noticed the organisation in the background". The more important the image projected to the outsiders involved in the project to you, then the more valuable these considerations are. It can therefore be expedient to make someone specifically responsible for looking after the outsiders before, during and after the workshop

Workshop language

The choice of the most appropriate project language is also part of the organisation of your CreativeTeam. As a basic rule: if not all of the people have the same native language, then English is most suitable as the workshop language. Most employees of international companies are used to working in English and English is also a language which is very suitable for CreativeTeams for a number of reasons: it is spontaneous, direct and informal, all factors which make for favourable dynamics in a team. Whichever language you decide upon: it is of central importance that the participants are fluent in it verbally and feel confident with it. Nowadays, this is not a problem with teenagers, they speak English almost as well as their native language; with other participants, if there are any doubts, then that person should be included who is most fluent in the project language. As an alternative, you can work with multi-language teams, which develop ideas in parallel: in a project for C&A with 13-year olds from all over Europe we had each group work in its own language and then communicate the results to the other groups using an interpreter. This a significant logistical effort, but in this case it was more important that the young people could speak in their native languages of German, Spanish, French, Dutch and English.

Generating too many or too few ideas

The duration of a CreativeTeam depends greatly on the complexity of the question and on the number of desired results. If, for example, you spend an hour just working on the question "which innovative distribution channels are there for our new line of cosmetics?", then you can assume that you will not generate enough material. You will have too few approaches to subsequently filter out really interesting ideas. That is because the question "distribution channels" contains very many different facets, and all of these facets need to be covered in the CreativeTeam.

If, on the other hand, you spend six hours collecting material on the subject "where do we want to go on this year's company outing?", then you can be sure that you will have too much information and will need much too much time in the condensing phase filtering the really good ideas out of the raw material. You need to think carefully about the length of time to be spent on generation for each question. For more trivial questions, 20 minutes is enough, for highly complex ones, eight hours is usually enough.

> **Core Concepts "CreativeTeam"**
>
> - For a CreativeTeam you need around 15 participants (insiders and outsiders) and a project leadership team, consisting of at least one moderator, someone to take notes and a steward, who looks after the food and drink and keeps the rooms tidy.
> - The room for the CreativeTeam should be able to hold four times as many people than will actually take part in the workshop. It should have natural daylight, access to the outside if possible and should be as different as possible to your usual daily work atmosphere. Mobile phones and laptops are locked away for the duration of the workshop; it makes sense to organise several short breaks each day for the usual office work to be carried out.
> - The questions (between four and 30, depending on how long the CreativeTeam should last) must be simple and linked to the appropriate technique. The techniques should be varied and motivate the participants to keep at it. The activities should last no longer than 15 minutes. Mix insiders and outsiders in each exercise.
> - Regular breaks, the right, healthy snacks, sufficient movement and the oxygen supply influence the quality of the results. Make sure the room is well ventilated and take a longer break after at most one hour, in which the participants can go outside.
> - Make sure that all results are properly noted and archived. You need each inspiration which has been collected for the subsequent condensing phase. Don't throw any material away.
> - Adjust the duration of the CreativeTeam to the complexity of the question; for very simple questions 20 minutes to two hours is enough; for questions with a medium level of complexity, two to four hours and for highly complex questions, six to eight hours. Avoid generating too little or too much material.

IdeaInterviews and ExpertInterviews

How to bring the ideas of many people on board

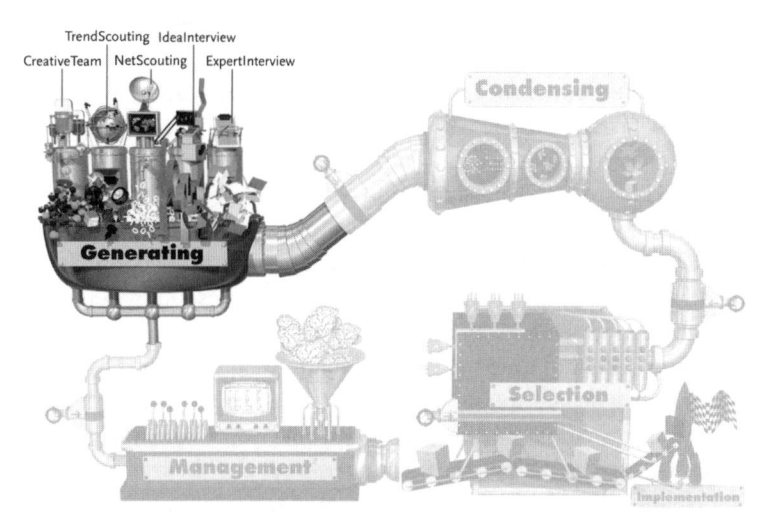

With IdeaInterviews and ExpertInterviews, you can enrich your ideas pot with important insights, needs and evaluations. Survey groups of three top experts up to 1000 IdeaTargets (the potential users of the idea) provide the required data.

All techniques in the industrial production of ideas serve a specific purpose. In the CreativeTeam, we look at the question intensively from a number of different perspectives; in TrendScouting and NetScouting, we look at other industry sectors and at other countries to come up with other ideas and IdeaInterviews and ExpertInterviews lead to ideas through an exchange with other people.

An exchange with other people is important because people always have ideas. But hardly anyone has practice in passing these ideas on to others. Here in Western Europe, the fear of sharing ideas is particularly prevalent; if someone has a good idea, then he usually keeps it to himself. We think perhaps "If it really was a good idea, then someone would already have implemented it a long time ago". Or we are scared of killer arguments or even of being ridiculed by our environment.

But it's not only ideas which are rarely passed on, the same applies to complaints, suggestions for improvement or opinions – all "sleeping ideas", or ideas with potential. We get extremely annoyed by bad service, but we usually only tell friends and acquaintances about it; or we are so irritated, that we decide not to spend one further minute in some hotline. But the person causing the irritation often has no idea what he's done. And he hardly ever receives a concrete suggestion on what he could do better in future.

And so there are – and certainly not only here in Europe – many people who carry good ideas around with them, but never pass them on. IdeaInterviews provide a possibility of capturing such ideas and integrating them into the idea project. Furthermore, questioning the IdeaTarget, the future user of the idea, fully corresponds to the approach of producing ideas industrially: you gather a lot of opinions in a short period of time to reach a result more quickly. It is more efficient to ask people about their ideas and wishes, than to work without this information. Furthermore, IdeaInterviews correspond to the "dare-to-share" principle: the more openly I deal with ideas, the more information I get back. And vice versa: the more ideas I keep to myself, the less I learn reliably from potential users as to what they think of it.

Market surveys usually take place very late in an innovation project: in such cases you can only really expect an "Okay" or a "No go" from the market, but no substantial contributions to enrich the idea. If, however, you approach the IdeaTargets with just an initial basic idea, then you can include their valuable feedback.

Asking people for their opinions

Ideas must always be judged by the target person who will at some point later be confronted with this idea. Depending on the idea concerned, a wide variety of groups of people obviously come into question. In our case, these have been small children, children and young people, employees of companies (from the lowest level to the top management), senior citizens, VIPs, investors, personnel managers, quality managers, engineers and many others, depending on the area in which the idea is being looked for. Interestingly, many companies are scared of this. It almost seems that they've lost interest in communicating with those people who will later use their ideas. But asking and asking again is an important part of the development of ideas: Are we going in the right direction with our idea? Will anyone want to buy, use and apply it later? Which corrections are necessary? Is the idea fun? What do you really want? What can we do better? Children have enough curiosity to ask questions. Let's be inspired by them and just cheekily ask.

There are always two components when you interview people: on the one hand, an evaluation of what already exists, including existing ideas, on the other hand, the question of further ideas. For this reason, IdeaInterviews can be carried out in various project phases. In the idea generation phase (see the diagram of the ideas machine at the beginning of the chapter), the main task is to find out the target group's needs, which can then be used as the basis for the development of ideas in the CreativeTeam, for example. In the condensing phase, interviews can be used to crosscheck the raw ideas which have been developed, and before implementation, it is vital to have the favourite idea which was chosen in the IdeaSelection validated.

Depending on the project, such interviews may have a more qualitative purpose, and they don't have to be representative in this case. In other cases, a quantitative survey based on representative samples will need to be made. In very many cases, the qualitative approach is perfectly adequate, and in your own idea production project, you will be in a position to carry out IdeaInterviews with 20 to 50 people yourself. If you make a representative survey, then you will probably need the assistance of a third party. You can use the following procedure in both cases.

Selecting your interview group

The first thing you need to do is to clearly define the group of people you want to interview. Who has something to say to your questions? Who must not be forgotten? Define your survey group (in market research, the term "sample" is also used), even if you only want to survey 20 people. It is important to mix the people to be surveyed, you should aim for the widest possible variety of people from your target group. If, for example, you need to interview young people between 13 and 19 in Hamburg and the surrounding area, then you should aim for the widest possible mix in that age group and also make sure that you have a good demographic mix (i.e. not all children from the same school, but some from the inner city, from the edge of town, from a wealthy area nearby and also young people who are doing an apprenticeship and no longer go to school). An example from Switzerland shows how important this is.

We wanted to test the idea of a youth ticket which we had developed for the Swiss Railways, SBB, directly with the target group, to get feedback from young people. We interviewed 100 young people from all over Switzerland, including some from Emmental, a remote mainly agricultural area. Five people were interviewed from this area. One question was "how would you like it if you could get a discount for the open-air festival with this card?". All five young people between the ages of 13 and 18, all questioned separately, had no idea what the term "open-air" meant. If we hadn't ensured that we had a representative sample then we probably wouldn't have learned that, even in Switzerland, not all young people are aware of a subject which is allegedly of so much interest to young people.

ExpertInterviews

Interviewing the IdeaTargets is not the only route to interesting components for your idea, it can also be very fruitful to ask experts. But, who are the right experts? Many people would probably immediately answer the question with "highly-qualified specialists who know a lot about a specific subject". And such experts can really be included. But not only them! It is unfortunately often the case, that the real experts, people who could contribute something significant to the subject are often completely excluded. In our project for the Swiss Railways, from which the product "Track 7" resulted, we suggested to the client, that the conductors of the trains should be included in the idea generation process and that we interview around

20 of them for their opinion on the ideas which had already been developed. The conductors were amazed that they were being asked for their opinion and one of us told us that it was the first time in his 20 years of employment that he had been asked for his opinion. These experts led us to the idea of using the youth product which the SBB was looking for in the area of evening travel from 7 p.m., because the conductors had told us about various problems they experienced in the evening: security problems, vandalism, women who disliked travelling alone in the evening. The final product provided a solution for everyone: the young people, who could travel free of charge after 7 p.m. and the SBB who could solve the security problem because the trains were no longer so empty after 7 p.m. The "experts" we interviewed were very grateful that they could share their needs with us and the important flow of information had been established. Therefore think carefully about who you really want to ask when you talk about experts!

There are various highly interesting categories of experts which we like to include:

1. Freaks: People who concern themselves with a specific subject, not necessarily professionally, but who know absolutely everything about it. These people often have their own homepage (for example, www.nokiasucks.com). Freaks have a unique perspective on a certain subject and can provide valuable information. However, you often have to check their sources and their opinions.
2. Retired experts: Many people who lived for a specific function the whole of their working lives are still fascinated when they retire if it concerns their personal expert subject. And so happy that someone is listening to them again at last. In our network, we have numerous older experts who have a lot of fun with our procedure and, additionally, are free of any obligations towards an employer. They can bring their expert opinion into our projects freely.
3. Researchers at universities, higher education colleges and in private companies and institutions: there is no subject on earth which no-one has never thought about. Every person who writes a doctoral thesis has been occupied with a certain subject over a long period of time and knows more about it than practically anyone else. These theses are open to the public, the authors are usu-

ally easy to find using modern research methods and are pleased to receive enquiries from companies and idea factories. People who work in research also often enjoy working on a task outside of their research radius for a change.

In a project for one of our clients, we had to develop an idea for a brochure on the subject of nutrition, for the target group of 20 to 30-year olds; the client liked the ideas so much that we were also directly asked to do the implementation. We set up an editorial team made up of young journalists who were supposed to put the ideas into words. One subject was "food in space" and Bianca, an 18-year old schoolgirl took on the subject: She considered how she could best find the necessary information. We explained to her that it would be best to talk to an expert, at best with an astronaut. "Of course let's ask Claude Nicollier!" Everyone agreed that the Swiss astronaut, who had fulfilled many missions for the NASA was the right man. Bianca immediately called him and Mr. Nicollier was delighted that someone was interested in what was eaten in space (and, above all, how). Including an expert is fascinating for both parties.

4. Another group of experts are the so-called "heavy users", people who use a certain service or a certain product particularly frequently. In a project for a Brazilian aircraft maker, for example, for whom we developed ideas such as how business jets could look in ten years time, we asked 250 frequent fliers about their needs and wants. It was amazing how many interesting statements these experts made which we would never have dreamt of. A frequent statement for example, was that the frequent fliers often prefer a quiet, relaxing flight to a flight with information, entertainment and food. Or that they would like to be able to hold a conference on short flights. Such statements from experts are worth their weight in gold for a project.

Preparing a survey concept

As soon as you know who you want to interview, then you should start to develop a survey concept. To do this, you think about the objectives you are following with the survey. The concept for the survey provides you with the basis for the questionnaire which you subsequently develop. In principle it is nothing more than a derivative of our old friend the project briefing (see the chapter "Briefing & Kick-Off"). It is about breaking down the subjects from the project briefing into those which could and should be dealt with in the survey.

Let's assume that your project task is to develop new ideas for services for business travellers in Europe. In the survey concept you determine the following points:

- When the survey should be carried out: you can develop the survey either before the development of initial ideas in the CreativeTeam (see the relevant chapter) or after the CreativeTeam. The difference is that in the first case you develop basic principles in the survey which you can use in the CreativeTeam, in the second case you have the possibility of confronting the people surveyed with the initial ideas. The choice of timing is therefore strongly dependent on what you want to achieve with the survey.
- The objective of the survey: what results do you want to see from the survey? In our example of the development of services for business travellers, for example, we wanted to get to know the needs of this target group and above, all, to learn what irritates them most about travelling today. The objective was to carry out a qualitative (not representative) study on the needs and irritations of business travellers from the most important companies in Switzerland.
- The size of the survey: determine which questions are to be answered by the survey and what assumptions you have about these questions. Assumptions are always made when developing a questionnaire to provide an orientation on the direction in which the questions should go. An example: I would like to find out in the survey which elements business travellers find most unpleasant when travelling. You develop certain assumptions, such as "waiting times at airports", "baggage", "impersonal hotels", "unhealthy food", "distance from friends and family", "being rushed", etc. In order to make the assumptions, you can talk to a representative of the target group to be surveyed. Create a script of the interview which shows how the questionnaire will basically be designed.

- Define exactly who you want to interview, meaning the detailed makeup of your sample. The size and the composition of the sample is highly dependent on the survey objectives.

The format of the questionnaire

When developing your questionnaire to ascertain the ideas of a specific group of people, you need to develop a standard format, made up of the headings Knowledge, Application, Opinion, Experience and Amusing Things. This format will help you to put together a questionnaire for IdeaInterviews quickly and uncomplicatedly, which is guaranteed to bring relevant results.

Remember: the industrial production of ideas is all about efficiency: You don't have to reinvent the wheel with every survey, but can rely on this format and then formulate additional questions where necessary. This format (see table below) is suitable both for evaluating existing ideas or products and for generating new ideas.

Heading	Evaluation level	New idea level
Knowledge	What do I know about fondues?	What do I want to know? What am I interested in?
Application	How do I make my fondue?	How would I prefer to make a fondue?
Opinion	What do I think of fondues? What do I think of the ideas I have been shown?	What would change my mind? Would the ideas I have been shown change my mind?
Experience	What has been my experience with fondues?	What experience would I like to have with fondues in future?
Amusing things	Funny things, curiosities, unusual things to do with fondues	Funny things, curiosities, unusual things to do with fondues

Table: Questionnaire format

Correct Question Technique

You can use different types of questions in a questionnaire. We use open questions, scaled questions, multiple-choice questions and yes-no-don't know questions.

- **Open questions:** In this type of question, the people interviewed have the possibility of answering as they wish. This question type is particularly suitable for asking for ideas which are "sleeping" within the interviewee. Open questions provide the interviewee with the greatest scope. You do, however, have to be aware that it is very demanding to evaluate these answers because it is difficult to fit them into categories. Therefore, use this type of question sparingly. Examples of open questions are: "If you could improve something in this idea, what would it be?" "What do you want from company X?"
- **Scaled questions:** Whenever the interviewees need to evaluate something, ideas, for example, or when they need to state their preference for something, then scaled questions are used. A scale between 1 and 10 is most useful. The scale can also be made up of smileys (for children for example) or of statements such as "applies fully to me", "applies somewhat to me", applies less to me", "does not apply to me". This form of question permits very exact evaluation as each response can be translated into a number.
- **Multiple-choice:** In this type of question, the interviewee selects one or more options from a list. This version is used when the interviewee can be shown a list of possibilities, for example, "Which mineral water do you prefer to drink?" Then you list all well-known mineral waters which are available on the market. Don't forget to add a line for mineral water which you have forgotten, so that the interviewee can add his preferred brand. Multiple-choice is a service to the interviewee, the person evaluating the responses and to the client, because it makes responding, evaluating, interpreting and presenting the results much easier.
- **Yes/no/don't know:** Some questions can be answered with a simple yes", "no" or "don't know", for example, the question "Do you know company XY?". These questions are designed to clarify

hard facts. There should, however, be no more than two or three of these questions in a questionnaire.

Testing the questionnaire and the concept, and selecting the interviewers

You should definitely pre-test the questionnaire on at least five people in order to find out if the questions provide the required answers, if they are simple and clear enough. With larger groups of people, the rule of thumb is that 5 percent of the total number to be interviewed should test the questionnaire before it is adjusted for a final time. It is a very personal matter to tell someone about your ideas and needs, no-one likes to think that the whole world is listening: personal interviews carried out by friendly people in a pleasant place, in a café for example, are therefore most suitable. It also makes sense to use interviewers who are close to the target group. There are psychological reasons for this: I will give significantly more open and authentic answers to someone who is similar to me than to someone whose whole being is foreign to me. The behaviour and appearance of the interviewer is of great importance for the relevance of the survey results. They must be instructed accordingly in advance. The interviewers need to know, not only what it is about, but also what they can expect on the other side. If, for example, customers of BMW are to be interviewed, then the interviewer should not wear jeans and arrive for the interview in her battered old VW Beetle. The interviewer should be knowledgeable about the local culture, i.e. the habits and behaviour in the country and conduct the interview appropriately. The creation of a friendly, trustworthy atmosphere, in which the interviewees feel at ease and secure is of particular importance. There is a different atmosphere whether I am interviewing a 13-year old boy or a 75-year old lady.

We never have our interviewers carry out more than ten interviews (with the exception of telephone interviews, which we only carry out when it is really urgent). As an interviewer, I can talk to ten people with interest and without routine and don't have to pretend to be interested when I'm not. The interview should also not be a strict working through of the questionnaire, but a conversation between two people where the interviewer can also read between the lines and make a note of additional information. Furthermore, it is polite to note the interview partner's questions and to let him have an answer – if necessary after referring back to the client – as quickly as possible.

It is also worth saying thank you to the interviewee with a small gift. Think of appropriate give and take. How valuable is the information which you get from your interview partner? In the case of IdeaExperts, for example, the fee could be a good case of Bordeaux (depending on the type of expert). For other interview partners, something which has to do with the subject of the interview and has a certain value would be suitable. Pure merchandising articles such as pens with the client's logo are therefore unsuitable and appear cold. We always discuss with our clients whether they want to provide the gift or whether we should organise something suitable. The interviewees are always pleased at such a small gesture – and the client makes a good impression.

Evaluating surveys

We enter the results of surveys in our BrainStore database, which presents all responses and is connected to the data from the rest of the idea generation process. With a smaller sample size, you can also make the evaluation using an Excel table. What is important is that you determine which interviewee made which statement, in order to be able to compare statistically interesting data such as the difference between the age groups or the sexes and other important data. Although we are, of course, interested in the facts and figures in IdeaInterviews and they do have an important meaning, we are mostly curious about and interested in individual responses. Such responses can completely throw a project off line because they can draw attention to a problem, provide a compelling argument for an idea or bring completely new ideas into the project. For that reason, a qualitative scan is first made by the project team, which can pick out such exceptional individual responses.

The statistical evaluation is then done using mean values and according to the polarisation of the responses (read more on this subject in the chapter "IdeaSelection").

Reporting the information

The evaluation of IdeaInterviews takes place at several levels:

1. A clear and attractive presentation of the facts and figures with all important breakdowns according to the demographic key of the survey group: what did the younger ones say, what did the older ones say? Do women have the same opinion as men? What about people who live in cities and those who are at home in rural areas? You find numbers people in every company, for whom the presentation of such figures is of huge importance and who immediately discover ideas and innovations in them. By the way: the evaluation can be attractive and stylish, it doesn't need to be in a completely dry form. Why not include pictures to show the content of the responses as well as tables and graphs?
2. Succinct, logical and comprehensible conclusions from the interviews in a short form. What are the key statements from the survey? This is particularly important for people who are not particularly interested in figures and who prefer to read a short, sharp fact.
3. A recommendation based on the results. This recommendation can be directly supported by the numbers and the key statements, but can also deviate from them. If all interviewees think an idea is fantastic and one person provides a killer argument against it, then the killer argument can destroy the whole idea. The recommendation therefore needs to be well-founded.

Core Concepts "Interviews"

- People have ideas. You just have to ask for them.
- Interview those people who will later be affected by the idea and put together a well-mixed sample from this group of people.
- Interview experts on the subject and remember that experts do not necessarily have to be highly-qualified specialists, but that freaks, retired people, researchers and heavy users may also be suitable.
- Make a concept showing the objectives of the survey and create a script for the interview.
- Create a questionnaire. The "knowledge, application, opinion, experience and amusing things" format may be helpful.
- Select the interviewees carefully and remember that people prefer to provide information to people who are similar to them. If you are interviewing young people, have young people carry out the interviews, if you are working with senior citizens, have older people carry out the interviews.
- Instruct your interviewers carefully concerning their task and give them behaviour guidelines. Ensure that interviewers do not just run through their questions, but create a friendly conversation in a pleasant atmosphere.
- Thank your interviewees with a small gift. Make a note of the questions posed by the interviewees and make sure that you get an answer quickly. That helps image building.
- Evaluate the results both qualitatively (interesting individual statements) and also statistically with figures. Break them down by demographic factors (for example, city/countryside, men/women, young/older) and show the demographic effects in diagrams.
- Prepare an evaluation with the figures, the key statements and a recommendation for the next steps.

TrendScouting and NetScouting

Taking a look over the garden fence will widen your horizons

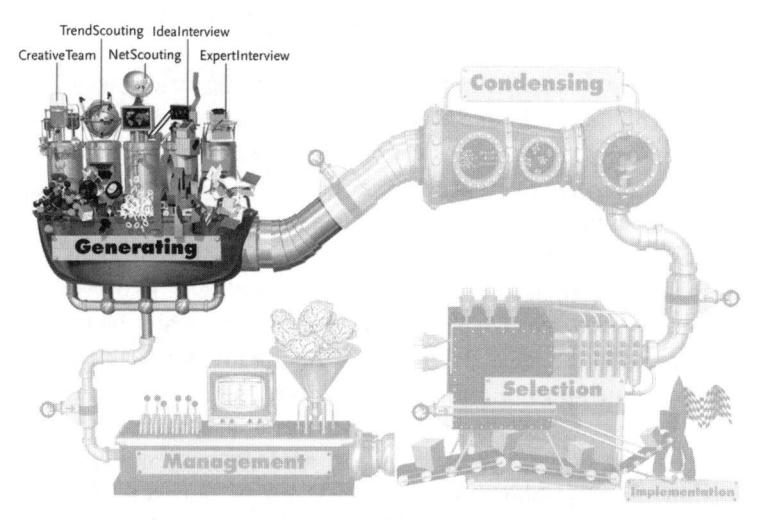

TrendScouting and NetScouting are techniques used in the idea generation phase. TrendScouting provides amazing ideas from various regions and industry sectors, NetScouting brings relevant input from the Worldwide Web in a very short period of time.

Imagine that you are the boss of a company which manufactures cosmetics and food. This combination has grown historically and both production series run in parallel without touching each other in any significant way. Now however, you find out from an international consumer research study, that today's consumers also expect, amongst other things, products which are exactly at the interface between cosmetics and food. A number of companies are already feverishly working on such products, which are already partly available in the market, for example, yoghurt with chunks of aloe vera. For you, as the CEO of this company, this is finally the chance to finally make use of the synergies between the two business areas. You commis-

The Idea Machine. Nadja Schnetzler
Copyright © 2005 WILEY-VCH Verlag GmbH & Co. KGaA, Weinheim
ISBN 3-527-50135-5

sion an idea factory to search for suggestions for products at the interface between cosmetics and food.

Our first component as an idea factory is the CreativeTeam made up of insiders and outsiders. The first peculiar, daring, new and amazing seeds of ideas and pieces of the jigsaw for new products at the food/cosmetics interface are developed there, a pot brimming over with ideas.

The second component is interviews. The needs and wants, suggestions and thoughts of a widespread group of consumers are surveyed and analysed. Pictures develop of everything which people can imagine on the borderline between cosmetics and food.

Both of these components are important. But something is missing: examples, exotic ideas, the international aspect. TrendScouting and NetScouting techniques can provide this. They widen the perspective and add unusual ideas to the idea pot. It often happens that a single input found in TrendScouting or NetScouting develops a whole new idea, which fits perfectly to the needs established in the survey and to the ideas developed in the CreativeTeam. But sometimes they just provide a different viewpoint on the problem which opens perspectives no-one would have dreamt of. TrendScouting also opens the eyes of many a customer who normally only develops incremental innovations. The product manager of a cat food brand, for example, for whom it is a really big thing if he can launch a new flavour with wild salmon instead of normal salmon. TrendScouting digs out the most unbelievable ideas for pet food from all corners of the world, from an energy drink for our four-legged fiends from Korea, toothpaste for dogs from the USA or dried pigs' noses from Scandinavia.

The CEO of the food/cosmetics company therefore suddenly finds innumerable products from a wide variety of countries, which show him possible interfaces between beauty and physical well-being, for example coconut milk, which is both drunk and used for personal care in Asia, bars from Japan containing aloe vera, vitamins from the USA which contain special components for skin regeneration and much, much more. What's special about this is not the examples of products as such, but the proof that yes, there are products on this borderline. We're not crazy to want to produce something like that.

TrendScouting has many different facets

The word TrendScouting can be confusing. The real purpose of TrendScouting is not to discover long-term trends at an early stage, but to use current trends and movements. The point is to create a portrayal of the current reality and mood, which can be used for orientation in the ideas project. A few examples will help to make this more clear:

Neckermann, the German catalogue retailer, was celebrating its 50th anniversary and asked BrainStore which interesting, unusual and unknown products could be offered in the Neckermann catalogue in the anniversary year. BrainStore sent TrendScouts to various cities, including Los Angeles, Tokyo, Mexico City and Sydney. In addition, NetScouting was done to find unusual products in the Internet. We found an unbelievable variety of things, from an underpants dispenser for 265 disposable underpants, a ball which you can stand in and roll down a hill, an inflatable mattress with integrated beer cooler to an olive oil spray (which has found its way into many kitchens in the meantime), in total over 300 product suggestions, each more peculiar than the next. The ideas were then added to with product suggestions from a CreativeTeam, which led to a catalogue with over 400 suggestions being developed.

Novartis wanted to develop an idea for a soft functional food, meaning a food which has an additional benefit for the body (a current well-known example being pro-biotic yoghurt drinks which strengthen the body's powers of resistance). In addition to a CreativeTeam and a survey of 250 consumers, we set off to look for products which have a function in various regions of the world. We found most products in Asia, amongst other things, a flour made of fish bones in Japan, which is supposed to be very good for bone growth and a drink from Korea called "Confidence" (a disgusting brew) which Koreans drink when they want to appear more self-confident (I've no idea if it actually works). It was this self-confidence drink which provided us with the idea, that a functional foodstuff doesn't necessarily need to have a physical function and that the function could also be psychological. The result of this was the idea of a breakfast product with the triple-action-formula, to feel beautiful, awake and happy first thing in the morning.

Mars (Masterfoods) was looking for ideas for new products for pets. What can you offer cats and dogs which isn't already available on the market? It was actually one of our private person clients which made us think about this question, she wanted to make an advent calendar for her four-legged friend before Christmas and asked us what it could look like. Through TrendScouting in Holland, the UK, the USA and Japan we found, amongst other things, slippers for dogs, oral care products for dogs, a cosmetic line for pets, hair colouring for dogs and cats and, of course, cigars for dogs (made of dog biscuits).

For the Swiss railway restaurant cars operator, we used TrendScouting to look for examples of mobile catering. We didn't discover anything really amazing anywhere in the world. This can also be an insight: there is nothing very fascinating available in the area of catering on the move. The question is: is that a reason not to do anything for the current client, or is that a reason to show some courage and provide amazing suggestions? The second option, of course. The problem was: when it came to it, our client had neither the courage nor the resources to implement the ideas, which is also the case with many other mobility providers.

We were asked to develop new baby food products by a baby food manufacturer. TrendScouting in the UK, the USA and France came up with a number of surprise products, amongst other things, finger food for babies (for example, mini sausages in a jar, which the baby can fish out itself and eat), dozens of versions of water (for example, "water with a hint of strawberry"), really strange combinations of cereals or toothache biscuits. This TrendScouting came up with many examples of products which you can buy in Switzerland today.

TrendScouting as a reward

TrendScouting is a much sought-after activity in our network and with our employees. The freelancers we use for it are people "between the worlds". They are people who know both the culture of our clients and the culture of the TrendScouting country. They notice unexpected and strange things much more quickly than people who live completely in the culture of one country. If you say to a Japanese person in Japan "find the 50 most exciting packaging forms in Tokyo's supermarkets", then he won't find anything useful, because he is used to everything. In Zurich however, a Japanese person will notice many things which a Swiss person won't see.

It's important that TrendScouts have their senses switched on and their eyes open, and that they are capable of working quickly and efficiently. The large number of impressions and diversions in TrendScouting mean that someone can very quickly lose his focus on the objective.

You can most certainly use TrendScouting in your team as an incentive for employees who you want to reward for good work. We also give our core team the opportunity to go on the TrendScouting hunt at regular intervals. On the one hand, this gives them some welcome variety, and, on the other hand, is a good control element for TrendScouting quality, with motivated team members who are allowed to have an exciting TrendScouting outing every now and again, you are guaranteed to get good results (but only if you give them precise instructions and a clear timeframe).

TrendScouting is like a journey into paradise for me. For once, I can buy everything which could be relevant to the client's project and send it back to BrainStore in huge boxes. Whenever we have a TrendScouting project, I usually try to cover one country myself. For TrendScouting provides us not only with ideas for clients' projects, but also basic inspiration, new perspectives and fresh approaches for our own work. At BrainStore, we always have a small exhibition of the weirdest products we found all over the world. My favourite things are a little bedside lamp from Dubai which shows the palace of the emir, yoghurt for dogs, oxygen spray with orange scent, soap with the aroma and texture of chocolate, a mousetrap called "Lucifer", a basket from South Africa made of telephone wires, an interpreter for dog language or a replica of a computer key, with the word "panic" on it. You're probably asking yourself what the purpose of all these objects is. The answer is simple: nothing. Although that's not quite correct. These objects awaken the desire to look at things in a different way. And that's exactly the perspective you need in your idea generation projects.

Good instructions, good results

Everything I already explained in the chapter "Briefing and Kick-Off", is also valid for TrendScouting instructions. The quality of the questions has a direct effect on the quality of the results. You need to precisely formulate what the TrendScouts should look for in order to get the results you hope for. An example of imprecise instructions would be "Look for interesting objects which Neckarmann could sell in their catalogue". An example of very precise instructions, on the other hand, would be:

- "Your task is to find, within 24 hours, as many objects, examples and photographs as possible from unusual and surprising objects, which in your opinion are not currently available in Germany. Please visit the following three locations: three supermarkets, two toy shops, two stationers, two hardware shops, two bookshops and eight other shops you notice. You can purchase products for a total of 500 US dollars. Please always buy two of each product and note the details of the product in your logbook. Label the product with a numbered sticker on which you note the object number from your logbook"

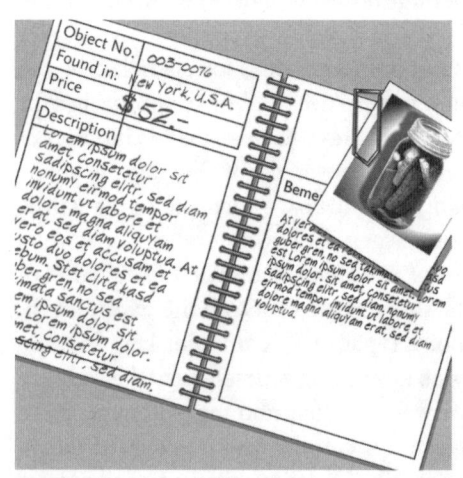

All the details of the object concerned are noted in the logbook: object number, what it is, where it was found, details/explanation, price.

TrendScouting and NetScouting

- If you think that some products could be explained by a photograph or a drawing, then make a photograph or a drawing and make a note of the details in your logbook. Transfer the digital photos to your laptop and label the photos with the number from your logbook.

The instructions need to be formulated that precisely so that no data gets lost. The TrendScouts are of course, available by phone if there are any queries, but the time between the receipt of all TrendScouting results and the point at which the results need to be evaluated is usually very short. It's quite possible for a TrendScout to collect up to 100 different objects and send back several hundred more observations and notes. These all need to be evaluated.

TrendScouting methods

As with CreativeTeams, various techniques are also used in TrendScouting to acquire the desired information. The techniques can be used individually or together, depending on the TrendScouting objective. We use the techniques TrendBuy, TrendTalk, TrendMag, TrendPhoto, TrendDescription:

- **TrendBuy:** Objects are bought from various locations, which could lead to good ideas for the project. Such locations can be supermarkets, bazaars, family shops, flea-markets, shops in train stations and any number of other places where products and services are offered for sale.
- **TrendTalk:** The TrendScout talks to people in the TrendScouting country about ideas: He is given a questionnaire, which he then works through with several people in a casual conversation. TrendTalk isn't really an interview, but a personal conversation in which new ideas from the country concerned can develop.
- **TrendMag:** Ideas are always also transported through magazines, journals or other publications such as cinema advertising, on television or in events. In TrendMag, the TrendScout systematically searches through as many publications as possible and marks and comments on the relevant things he finds.

- **TrendPhoto:** In TrendPhoto, the TrendScout takes photographs of good ideas and input. This is particularly the case if the idea cannot be bought or described in simple terms. Examples could be: unusual products and services (India: the ear cleaner who goes from house to perform personal oral hygiene, USA: really peculiar restaurant designs) or ideas where a picture says more than a thousand words.
- **TrendDescription:** Behaviour, systems and interdependencies, which cannot be photographed or physically transported are described using this tool (for example: "special rates at the cinema every Monday" or "50 percent of the women in Paris walk around with a bottle of Evian under their arm").

Idea mining

Evaluating TrendScouting is a lot of fun, and a lot more work. All objects and notes, which usually arrive in Fed-Ex packages at our office, first need to be unpacked and sorted. We have had TrendScoutings projects for which we had to hire an additional room to lay all the material out in. A sports hall is extremely suitable in such cases, you have a lot of space there.

Once you've laid out all the material, all the objects are sorted into subject clusters. Things which are connected by subject are put together. Finally, the objects are photographed and the corresponding description and catalogue entry entered in the database. A report can now be printed from this database which shows all objects and the subject clusters. Objects or ideas which fit to an existing idea from a different project phase (CreativeTeam, IdeaInterview) are immediately allocated to it.

The objects are stored in boxes until they are used in one of the following project phases. At the end of the project, they are stored in labelled boxes. But take care not to keep food items for a long period of time; we once made this mistake and bitterly regretted it in a clean-up session. You can, of course, have an auction of the amusing objects at the end of TrendScouting or hold an exhibition for your employees.

NetScouting

As with TrendScouting, the aim of NetScouting is to enrich your pot of ideas with international ideas and examples. Everyone knows how much useful information can be found in the Worldwide Web yet it is still amazing. Nowadays, many companies are much more free with their information in the Web than in other channels (annual reports, press conferences, etc.). There are thousands of pages on every subject in the Web.

But the Internet is like a goldmine: only trained personnel will be able to bring the precious metal from the gallery up to the surface, the others will only find dirt. It is therefore important, that NetScouting is only done by people who know what they are doing and are absolute experts in looking for information. It's not enough to know the code of one or more search engines. Talent, training and the right tools are necessary to filter the valuable information out from the huge number of possible information suppliers. If you would like to carry out NetScouting, then I would recommend outsourcing it to a professional provider; at BrainStore, we benefit from our international network and from many freelancers who have grown up with the Internet and some of whom really do know all the tricks to get the desired information out of the Internet. Depending on the subject, a combination of skills may be wanted, for example, a competent Internet surfer with graphic design training to search for examples of graphically appropriate sites if the project is concerned with finding good examples for current graphic design for an idea. Or a competent Internet surfer, who knows about psychology for the search for Internet sites where the visitors are addressed in a psychologically clever way.

NetScouting is best split by language: English is obligatory, after that the decision needs to be made on which language areas have something to contribute to the desired subject; these sites then need to be searched by people who know the language concerned on suitable computers (or can your computer create texts in Arabic?). You do, of course, need people who are capable of also translating and interpreting the sites which have been found.

The preparation of a clear briefing is also the most important preparatory task in NetScouting. Give the NetScouts brief background information on the entire project and then describe the objectives of the NetScouting phase. What do you want to look for? What kind of information are you interested in (if possible, provide an example) What are you not looking for (an example can be helpful here also)? Define a clear timeframe for the search and stop the search at the end of that time.

It's important that the NetScouts always provide the following information:

- Screenshot (digital photo) of the Internet page the found,
- URL (address) of the Internet page the found,
- Details of the relevant information on the page (for example, "unique form of online purchasing thanks to a special database structure").

Evaluating NetScouting

All pages which are found are put into a file with a detailed description. The IdeaManager puts together a summary of the most important findings and makes it available to the idea team for the idea condensing phase together with the files containing the findings. Interesting findings or clear cross-references to existing ideas are noted directly in the database of the idea concerned. For example, in an idea generation project which is concerned with developing possible forms of childcare by employers, the idea of parents and children having lunch together comes up. The NetScout finds a number of examples online of companies who provide exactly that. All URLs of these companies and a short description of what is provided are noted on the original idea and a cross-reference is made to the relevant page in the NetScouting file. That makes overview and access much easier.

However, you are not just looking for that kind of cross-reference; independent, new ideas can be found in NetScouting and TrendScouting. Both things are important: on the one hand, NetScouting and TrendScouting can support, enrich or destroy existing ideas, on the other hand, they can also bring missing or new ideas into the process. In either case, they ensure that exotic and international input is also considered.

There are a number of reasons for carrying out TrendScouting. A few typical examples of projects in which TrendScouting (and always NetScouting as well) makes sense are:

- The development of a new product: examples and models of all components of the new product can be looked for, from the packaging or the contents, to the marketing. TrendScouting provides many interesting product samples from all over the world which can be used in the phase of condensing ideas.
- Finding new business areas: unusual products, new companies and ideas for services are available everywhere in the world and just need to be found. TrendScouting and NetScouting can complement the local perspective and unexpected ideas can develop.
- Solving a structural problem: if the subject is improving or adjusting processes and structures, then NetScouting in particular can provide valuable additional information; companies like to present their new and innovative processes and procedures in the Internet and cite examples. Academic studies, papers and models on the required subject can be found easily, which can then be included in the idea generation process. Examples of such subjects are recruitment of employees, new employment models, employee and customer satisfaction, industrial psychology, internal training and development, logistics and much more.

You should calculate at least five days per country for the preparation, carrying out and evaluation of TrendScouting, (not including the search for the TrendScouts). The preparation takes one day, TrendScouting one or two days, the sending of the material with DHL or Fed-Ex 24 hours, the evaluation one day. Calculate a further half day for each additional country which is worked by additional TrendScouts.

Experience has shown that it is worth setting up a 24 hour hotline for the TrendScouts in case they have questions. As we work with very young TrendScouts at BrainStore, who sometimes also need advice on very practical matters (stolen passport, money spent and other niceties), it goes without saying that we provide this. But sometimes the Scouts also have important questions on content, which lead to a badly carried out commission if they're not answered quickly. And if you think that you need to calculate around 5,000 Euros per country for TrendScouting, then that doesn't make sense.

> **Core Concepts "TrendScouting and NetScouting"**
>
> - TrendScouting and NetScouting are suitable for letting exotic and international ideas flown into the project or finding examples from other countries.
> - TrendScouting provides product samples, magazine articles, photos or descriptions from a certain cultural circle on the subject of the project. NetScouting searches for interesting examples, models or statements in the Internet.
> - You need specialists for both disciplines: for TrendScouting, the most suitable people are those who know both your culture and the culture of the TrendScouting country very well and are capable of discovering amazing ideas. For NetScouting you need Internet freaks, who have perfect command of all search techniques, follow instructions and are fluent in the language of the country in which NetScouting is to be carried out.
> - The more exact your instructions, the more interesting the results will be: give your TrendScouts and NetScouts focused instructions, which are free of any misunderstanding and clear directions on the filing and structuring of the material.
> - When you have received the material from all TrendScouts, sort it by subjects and document it in minute detail. Assign obvious ideas which fit to the ideas which have already been developed, directly to those ideas. Prepare the remaining material in such a way that it can be used in the ThinkTank phase.

IdeaCity and ThinkTank

How to turn quantity into quality

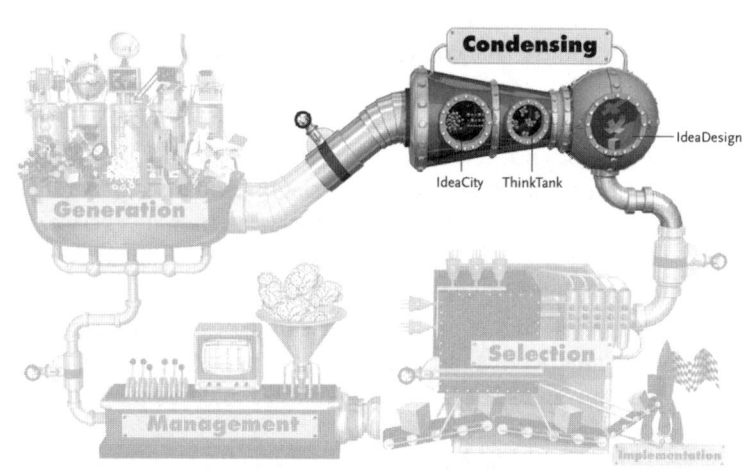

IdeaCity and ThinkTank are steps in the condensing of ideas. Finished ideas are made from the pieces of the jigsaw puzzle which you collected in the idea generation phase.

A large hospital was looking for ideas with us on getting the right applicants for jobs in the care area more easily and quickly. In the middle of the workshop, after a tremendously fast idea generation phase, our client, the manager of the personnel department suddenly said with consternation: "But how are you going to find the right idea from all the ones we have generated? It's like looking for a needle in a haystack!"

We have experienced this kind of uneasiness on many occasions. Many of our clients are a little afraid of the large quantity of data which we come up with in the idea generation phase. After using the tools CreativeTeam, TrendScouting and NetScouting, plus IdeaInterviews and Experts, that can be up to 10,000 raw ideas, which we have to reduce to just a few good ideas in the subsequent condensing phase. People aren't used to that. Most people seem to find it more logical to deal with a little information thoroughly than to speed through a lot of information.

Instinctively, that's completely correct, our brain really isn't capable of processing such large quantities of data meaningfully. But no-one is asking one person to juggle with 10,000 idea fragments alone – there's an appropriate team, an appropriate procedure and appropriate technical support for that. This is where the approach of producing ideas industrially comes into effect: the ideas are systematically condensed using an optimised process. And the thorough work with a few ideas, the careful evaluation, consideration and discussion happens too – but not yet!

At BrainStore, after our initial experiences with idea generation projects we very quickly came to the conclusion, that it is very easy, safe, successful and efficient to make an enormous quantity of inspirations available to a suitable and well-mixed team – much better than having a few highly-paid specialists brood over a limited number of well thought out approaches after having been told to "find an idea!", with a significant risk that they will not develop any usable ideas in the short time available.

The large quantity of data serves as a kind of "extended brain" in which the team can look for those inspirations which are most suitable for the project. The task is now not "be creative!", but "pick out of all the available inspirations, those seeds of ideas which could serve the project and combine them appropriately". We're concerned therefore, with suitable selection, not with a creative act.

This extended brain is also useful because the inspirations and idea fragments come from many very different people from our CreatingCommunity. People with different interests and experience, from various regions and age groups. After a good idea generation phase, we can therefore assume that we have a really interesting mix available, a much wider starting point than would usually be possible in a company or department.

Colourful teams are not only useful in the idea generation phase. They are also advantageous in condensing ideas. Every person approaches this huge, bubbling pot of ideas in a different way, everyone scans from their own personal perspective: the marketing specialist looks from a marketing viewpoint, the young person looks for striking ideas, the customers looks for useful things and so on. Additionally, everyone has their own personal strengths and each person prefers to work with different techniques. There are people who prefer visual stimulation, others prefer acoustics, and still others need to discuss it beforehand in order to get good results. The question is: how do we enable the participants to use this data pot, this "extended brain" meaningfully? In the first phase of condensing ideas, we use a few simple, but plausible procedures and techniques: we call them IdeaCity, FirstScan and CriteriaScan, Lavalamping and ThinkTank.

The city of ideas

We call the virtual place where we carry out the first phase of condensing ideas IdeaCity. All inspirations from the idea generation phase can be examined by all team members in this city. For this purpose, we have fed all the ideas generated into our database the very minute they were developed and have sorted them according to various key words where necessary. Results from market research, TrendScouting or ExpertInterviews have been prepared and made accessible using graphics, posters or projection shows, for example. Everyone now has access to these inspirations in the IdeaCity, using various channels:

- **Cinema:** All inspirations move slowly and gently across a large screen in random sequence. The observer can see them all and pick out those which interest him.
- **Museum:** Three-dimensional inspirations, pictures, posters and everything which can't be integrated into the database can be exhibited in the museum. The observer can meander from one place to the next and let himself be inspired by the objects (which are also labelled and described).
- **Bar.** Those people who like to get straight into the data (which is true for me for example), can sit at one of our networked laptops and look at the inputs from the database there in order to melt them into new ideas.

- **Garden:** The participants find themselves in a garden atmosphere in one of the other locations. Those people who like to discuss ideas can retire to the garden with the IdeaBook (a printout from the database) and discuss new ideas.
- **Bath:** Small tickets on which the individual inspirations from the database are printed lie in a huge bathtub. Highly suitable for people who like to rummage around and pick out and develop ideas based on chance.

The objective of the city of ideas is to make the existing pot of ideas, which is filled with around 3,000 inspirations in an average project, shrink to around 5 percent of its volume, which, in an average project, means 150 to 200 ideas. In addition to the various possibilities of viewing the idea material, we also make various methods and experts available to the participants (at this stage, still a mix of insiders and outsiders).

The exact formulation of the question which we devised in the briefing together with the client for example. Whereas this question only appeared in passing or hidden in the prepared questions for the workshop during the idea generation phase, it is now the focus of attention. At the beginning of IdeaCity, the moderator points out that the objective is now to create ideas from the inspirations form the CreativeTeam and the other tools, which answer the question. Every participant therefore receives a ticket with the exact formulation of the client's question, a kind of compass for his visit to IdeaCity.

Three people with special functions are available to the participants in this phase: the *writer*, the *combiner* and the *illustrator*. The *writer* has the task of collecting the ideas which the participants have written by hand on A4 sheets and entering them into the database, if the participants don't want to do so themselves. The *combiner* looks after participants who have found two interesting components for an idea and would now like to combine them but aren't sure how. He discusses various directions the combination could take with them and then also enters the idea into the database. And the *illustrator* makes sketches and illustrations when the participants think that the idea would be easier to understand with an illustration. The illustrations are scanned and added to the database of ideas.

As opposed to the Creative Team, where we were concerned with speed and quantity, the emphasis in the IdeaCity is on quality and more contemplative work. Whereas in the previous phase, dynamic youngsters pushed the managers to top performance, the participants now work peacefully together, discuss, exchange and note ideas. We often see new alliances take place here: as the insiders and outsiders have already got to know each other a little, they see each other with new eyes when they meet in this phase. The youngster is suddenly an expert for the manager and the manager is suddenly an interesting discussion partner for the youngster who previously found him boring. But we don't force conversations: if anyone wants to set off alone on the hunt for ideas, then there is nothing him stopping him from doing so. We from BrainStore also set off hunting and look for particularly promising ideas which we noticed with a practised eye and feed into the system ourselves.

I can give you an insight into this stage in the process using an example: the aim of the project with our client Rolex was to communicate three management values, which the Board had defined for its management team, to that team in a pleasant and astonishing way in a 45 minute event. The three values were not only to be communicated intellectually, but were to be anchored deep within the management team. The three values were "be a role model", "act like an entrepreneur" and "respect people and things". In the CreativeTeam, we examined the question formulation from 24 different perspectives, amongst others:

- How can you hold the attention of a group of people for 45 minutes?
- If you were a circus director, what would be your next sensation?
- What do you give someone in order that he remembers you for a long time?
- What do parents do with their children to stop them arguing?
- What can be learned in the subject "being a role model" and how does the teacher communicate the material?

The combiner, illustrator and writer help the participants in the IdeaCity to combine, illustrate and formulate their ideas.

126 | IdeaCity and ThinkTank

After three hours work, there were over 3,000 seeds of ideas in the ideas pot, amongst other things, statements like "cleaning teeth", "three values – three colours", "entrance of the juggler", "brainwashing", "designing sculptures", "riding a tandem", "design an advertising poster", "sing together", "experience a ritual together" and, of course, a lot more things.

In IdeaCity, a participant is now confronted with the statement "sing together" or "brainwashing" for example. He finds both of these statements interesting and combines them, either by himself or with the help of the "combiner", to the idea "the team develop a song together on the subject of the three values and record it professionally in a recording studio. The song is played frequently and all employees (not only the management team) are given a CD. He enters this idea into the database himself or gives it to a "writer" who enters it for him (this service is particularly appreciated by older participants who have a few problems with the speed of the process).

Another person perhaps sees the ideas "juggling" and "assign a different colour to each value". That develops into the idea "each of the three values is assigned a colour. Every employee is given three juggling balls and a basic course in juggling. Now he can juggle with the three values every day".

The roles "writer", "combiner" and "illustrator" are not a precondition for the success of your IdeaCity. What is much more important is that you look at the ideas from different perspectives with your team and create new, concrete ideas from them. You can guarantee this by presenting all of the inspirations from the CreativeTeam clearly and in different forms.

An IdeaCity session lasts between 15 minutes and four hours depending on the quantity of inspirations which have been generated. If the team has been made up of a good mix of people, then between 40 and 500 different ideas will be developed which are now ready for the next phase in the condensing of ideas: the IdeaScans. As you can see in the Rolex example, the ideas have now been formulated in a more concrete way, but they are still only semi finished goods. The ideas will become increasingly concrete in the next few steps.

FirstScan and CriteriaScan

The amazing thing about the idea machine is that up to this point in time we haven't had to think about things like feasibility, killer expressions, hierarchies or other unnecessary questions: a great privilege! That doesn't however mean that we've been working chaotically and without any objectives. We have circled in on the client's question, illuminated it from several sides and then sorted and recombined the material which has been collected and created the initial seeds of ideas which are now ready to be put though the big idea filter. Now's also the time to say goodbye to the large team. A new team is needed to select the ideas, but also one which represents different perspectives. It includes:

- Criteria experts, i.e. people who are capable of evaluating the ideas which have been found against the project criteria which were determined in the KickOff. They are recognised experts in the appropriate field. At least two people per criteria (usually a main criterion and two ancillary criteria) should be consulted. The experts can come from within the company or outside it.
- Lateral thinkers who simply are of the basic opinion that "everything is possible". These are usually people who have worked for several years in project management, events or conceptual work or who run their own companies, people who have to create something new every day.
- Idea experts who know the process of the industrial production of ideas and can categorise and allocate ideas from this perspective.

The purpose of FirstScan, is to evaluate the seeds of ideas which come out of IdeaCity and to decide if they

- can remain in the idea pot,
- should be thrown out
- or need to be changed

There is still room for completely new suggestions in this phase. We don't throw anything away either, we just make an inventory of the opinions of our insiders and experts. Our BrainBase (our database application) does the calculations for us, but you can, of course, do it by hand by asking your participants to give points to each idea. Or you can work with a simplified data solution, such as an Excel table for example.

This first scan is very raw and also quite emotional. The killer expressions can appear here and are allowed to do so and it's quite possible that someone will sweep some ideas from the table with a "absolute rubbish" or "we've had that before". It can however also happen, that someone else in the team finds such an "absolute rubbish idea" extremely interesting and sees much more in it which could be developed (there is a commentary area for this in the FirstScan). So it is still a multidisciplinary, colourfully mixed team at work, which also gives polarising outsider ideas a chance and not only the mainstream ideas which anyone could have come up with.

An example of one such successful outsider idea was a product which we developed for Novartis. The task was to develop a "soft functional food", a foodstuff which would fulfil a function above and beyond its nutritional characteristics, which the consumer would benefit from. This sounds abstract, but was highly exciting in the project, we came up with a wide variety of suggestions. One of them for example, was a vegetable bar, which has a positive effect on the digestion, another was a ginger-honey lolly with guarana, which you eat after a meal, which freshens the breath and wakes you up. The polarising outsider idea which remained in the idea pot, although not everyone liked it, was a breakfast drink with three functions: it makes you feel awake, beautiful and happy.

This idea appeared absurd and risky at first sight, and we could have been tempted to ban it from the idea pot with a killer expression. But the IdeaManager in the project defended the product vehemently and kept providing proof that the time was ripe for such a product. And the desire to feel awake immediately in the morning, to feel beautiful and satisfied had, in fact, come up several times in the CreativeTeam and the IdeaInterviews which we had carried out with 250 consumers. The idea "beautiful, awake, happy" finally asserted itself – and was launched onto the market as "Ocléa" a breakfast drink with the triple action formula.

The necessity of such polarising ideas can also be seen clearly in the development of names. I wasn't present at the time, but I think that names such as Kodak or Häagen Dazs, both of which are strong international brands, would hardly have had a chance, if they had had to assert themselves democratically in a classic idea generation project as it takes place in companies today. I rather think that these names were "made" by strong personalities and were suddenly just there. At BrainStore, polarising ideas have a good chance of staying in the final selection. Polarising ideas are important: they rub people up and get talked about.

Furthermore, the fact that you find an idea dubious, or even stupid at first sight, says nothing about its quality. I'm constantly amazed how ideas which our clients at first reject, then suddenly do grow on them. Another example of finding a name, because that is where emotions run highest: the largest Swiss college of communication and marketing, SAWI, formed an education cooperation with other colleges of higher education on the subjects of communication, marketing and business. The cooperation was to provide centralised education packages. This education platform needed a name. Among many other suggestions, BrainStore presented the name Edwin or ed.win, from education and win. The name was fresh, provocative and very personal. It came off very badly at first in the client's evaluation. Someone even wrote on the evaluation form "Edwin? We might as well call it John!" It looked as though Edwin was out of the race. But wrong: during the presentation, the name Edwin kept coming up and at the end of the meeting, the majority of the participants had moved over to support Edwin. The first jokes started as people were leaving the conference room "Don't forget to give Edwin a call" or "I go to school with Edwin". A good name provides good topics of conversation and a topic of conversation had been found here. It takes courage of course, to offer a suggestion which so obviously polarises, but if we ourselves are convinced that we would be doing our clients a service with it, then it's not difficult to find that courage.

Our BrainBase database therefore consciously leaves polarising outsider ideas in the system – even after initial rejection. An idea only disappears completely after this phase if it is thrown out of the pot by everyone. If a single person wants to keep it in the pot, then that's where it stays, with few points, however.

Ideas are emotionally filtered in the FirstScan and systematically checked for compatibility with the briefing in the CriteriaScan.

The CriteriaScan takes place almost immediately after the FirstScan: this filtering process examines all ideas against the criteria developed at the beginning of the project: You remember: one main criterion and two ancillary criteria. The participants therefore now filter all ideas first according to the main criterion, then according to the first ancillary criterion and then the second ancillary criterion. They have to evaluate on a scale from one to ten how well each idea meets the criteria. The system calculates the results and comes up with a statistic. This statistic now shows all ideas in an overview, in two views:

1. An overview of the ideas in a ranking list: which idea has been given how many points?
2. An overview of the polarisation of the individual ideas. How strongly do the various evaluations of the participants diverge from the average?

These two overviews are a systematic stocktaking of the previous work: all the energy which has gone into these ideas is now shown in two tables – the basis for the continuation of the work in the Think-Tank.

ThinkTank, Part 1: LavaLamping

Do you know what lava lamps are? They are those futuristic, cylindrical lamps in which a coloured liquid and brightly-coloured balls float around, which continuously separate and rejoin other balls. The effect of warmth makes something amazing happen in these lamps: the bubbles rise and fall, join up with others, separate. That's exactly what happens in the next step in the idea machine with the ideas which are still in the pool, that's why we call the process LavaLamping.

The same participants take part in this stage as in the two filter processes FirstScan and CriteriaScan. The process is led by an experienced moderator. Every participant is given a printout of the ranking and the descriptions of the ideas and can at first occupy himself with them on his own. Then each idea is discussed briefly, the arguments for and against them are stated.

The experts provide their view of things, the specialists from BrainStore ask important questions: How can that be done? Has that already been tried? Who knows more about it? What could make us fail? All information is stored. The idea is gradually refined using new argumentation, arguments and continuous adaptation and a detailed description of the idea results.

At this stage, combinations of ideas often develop which were previously separate; it's also interesting that ideas which appear absurd or weird at first sight, keep coming up to the surface during LavaLamping. We call these ideas "troublemakers" uncomfortable ideas which don't let go of you very easily. Such ideas often circulate around all participants. First you find them stupid, then, suddenly highly interesting, finally perhaps completely wrong again. I remember one such idea, which we still laugh about today and we still haven't really let go of, although no one has yet implemented it: the idea for a game to be played in trains, where figures moving past in the countryside had to be "shot" with a mobile phone. If I press the right button on my mobile phone at the right time i.e. when I am in game mode, then the "trophies" are credited to my game account. The winner is the person with the most "trophies". This game can be played alone or in groups. This idea kept coming up to the top during a LavaLamping session for a mobile communication provider. The client, who found it terrible at first, said "No", then let himself be convinced by an expert that the idea would be a hit. Suddenly, everyone only wanted to talk about this idea. On the other hand, the IdeaManager was sceptical and said the idea wasn't suitable as a mass game and wouldn't make a profit either. The trophy game was talked about over and over again during the whole of the LavaLamping session and although it wasn't implemented, it won a place in the list of ideas to be presented – only if just to make the spirits rise.

A LavaLamping session needs to be carefully moderated and the feelings and inclinations of the individual participants mustn't distract the moderator from the real task in hand: to find good ideas which correspond to the objectives and criteria of the client. The objective of LavaLamping is to find ten to 20 such ideas. A LavaLamping session lasts between one and six hours depending on how complex the project is.

ThinkTank, Part 2

A BrainStore team, which includes selected experts, now puts the finishing touches to the ideas. Every idea is examined in detail and a list made of all the questions which need to be answered: Who can do it? How do we make that possible? How does it work exactly? Which problems could arise? How could this idea be made even better? And so on and so forth. Depending on the type of project, this work lasts between a few hours and several days. The objective is to filter out those ideas which do not fit to the client's briefing, cannot be implemented or if so, then only with a huge amount of effort or which are already used by the competition. The client is given an initial guideline on implementation with the ideas which are accepted.

Feasibility studies, tests, discussions with experts and a search for potential implementation providers are part of this work. Whether this clarification is of a general nature or more detailed depends on the amount of time and the budget which are available for the idea. At the end of the ThinkTank, each idea is described on an A4 sheet. The same basic rule also applies to the ThinkTank if it is to be successful: it is decisively important that it is made up of the correct mix of people. The CreativeCommunity needs to provide its best people with their concentrated specialist knowledge – but without coming up with a team of divas; the experts and specialists need to work as a team and regard their own ideas and their own image as of secondary importance.

Experts from the client's side should always be present. Depending on the project, we either include the ProjectOwner (the client who commissioned the idea) in the ThinkTank or do without him. This is a difficult and important decision. A ThinkTank can be an explosive mixture and things don't always go as smoothly in the ThinkTank as they do in the other stages of production. There are heated debates, disagreements and many, many questions. Not all clients can cope with these dynamics and at the same time take part in the discussions and keep up their optimism that a really good result will come out of it at the end. Other clients are used to such discussions and fit well into the team, also because of their expert view. It is vital to have not only the right team and the right moderation, but also the right rhythm with a lot of breaks. This absorbs dead moments where ideas suddenly seem to be destroyed. And many an idea rises like a phoenix from the ashes after such a regenerating break.

The last step in the ThinkTank is the preparation of the briefing for the IdeaDesigner. Which style and which pictorial ideas should these ideas use to show the ideas in comparison to each other? How should the ideas be made clear to our client? And so the ThinkTank moves smoothly into the next subject, IdeaDesign.

Core Concepts "IdeaCity & ThinkTank"

The following steps are necessary to develop good ideas from a large number of inspirations:
- Prepare information in such a way that outsiders can examine and analyse it.
- Examine and analyse the inspirations from the idea generation phase in relation to the idea briefing. Use a team of insiders and outsiders, preferably the same people as in the CreativeTeam, for efficiency reasons. Give the participants the possibility of looking at the inspirations from several perspectives and using various instruments and discussing them. Each participant should develop at least 15 suggestions of his own.
- Filter and evaluate all the remaining suggestions in two rounds: a) an initial emotional filter, where it is spontaneously decided whether the idea remains in the race or not; and b) a criteria filter, where the ideas are evaluated against the main criterion and the ancillary criteria from the idea briefing. Make sure you keep ideas in the race which not everyone likes.
- All ideas which are left at the end of this filtering process need to be discussed and assessed in detail, under the leadership of an experienced moderator who can take up and summarise the various positions and bring the ideas up to the next level. Make sure there are enough breaks.
- Discuss and research the basic feasibility of all ideas. Describe them in a detailed and clear way (maximum one A4 sheet). Prepare the briefing for the IdeaDesign (how are these ideas to be shown and communicated both visually and with regard to content? See next chapter).
- The team is of decisive importance for the success of the ThinkTank: think about which specialist areas and experts are important for the ThinkTank; only invite those experts who are prepared to work in a team and consider whether the client (the ProjectOwner) should be included in the ThinkTank or not.
- The ThinkTank should take place in a quiet place which is as free from interruptions as possible. If you don't have an idea factory yourself, suitable locations are, for example, conference hotels, ships (reserve a separate conference room), mountain huts (with telephone reception), school rooms, restaurants (reserve a separate room) or any other room where you won't be followed by your daily business.

IdeaDesign

How ideas can be compared, made easy to understand and durable.

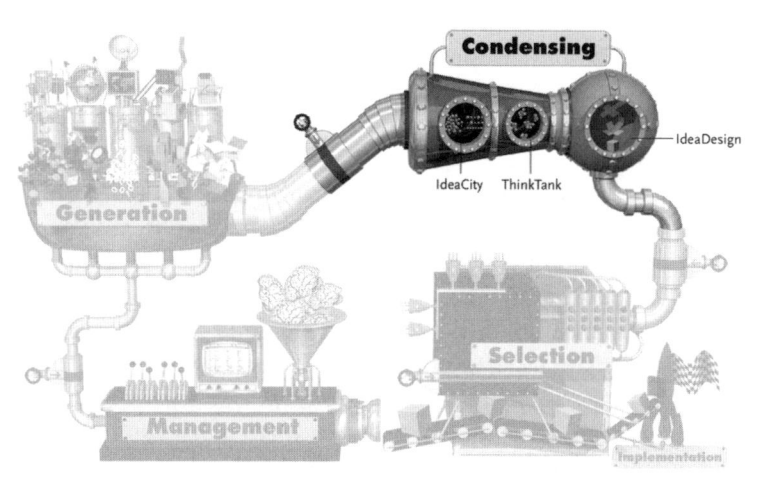

IdeaDesign is the last stage in the phase of condensing ideas. Here, the ideas are put into a form which enables them to be compared, easily understood and durable.

You have no doubt already taken part in innumerable meetings in which ideas have been presented and discussed. Let's assume that this time the question is how your company should present itself at the next trade fair. A meeting is called in which a number of suggestions are discussed. The marketing manager and a trainee from the sales department have some ideas which they would like to present. The marketing manager presents his idea full of self-confidence and makes a presentation which his secretary worked on for several days. He dazzles with facts and figures, graphics and pretty pictures. He has printed a summary for all participants which he presents in an attractive folder. The trainee from the sales department doesn't have as much experience in making presentations and presents her ideas verbally, by shyly reading from a handwritten notepad. She appears unsure and doesn't formulate her ideas very clearly.

Which idea will receive most attention? Most certainly the marketing manager's, for a number of reasons: his seniority and position in the company give him weight; he is the more credible sender. His presentation is interesting and well-designed, its form is convincing. With regards to the content, then he has more experience of which statements, facts and information are more relevant for the company. The trainee may present better ideas when looked at objectively, but she will still fail as the sender, because the form of her presentation is unprofessional and the contents – because they are probably not targeted on the needs of the company – are irrelevant.

The sender, form and contents are therefore important for the evaluation of an idea. If you want to find out which of the various ideas which are left over after the condensing phase of an idea generation project are better or worse, then you first need to put them into a uniform form concerning appearance and contents. Ideas can't be compared until then. And they don't become easy to understand and durable until then either. Durability and comprehensibility are two decisive factors for the value of the end result of an idea generation project. When I see ideas which we developed and visualised many years ago, I never cease to be amazed that I still understand the idea immediately with no further explanation and out of context. Even people who had nothing to do with the development of the idea are capable of explaining it to others – thanks to the Idea Design.

My favourite idea, which I like to tell potential clients about, was developed without any involvement on my part and I have never studied the detailed documents about the idea, but it is just so brilliantly shown that everyone understands it immediately. The aim of this project was to develop ideas for the public transport operators in Zurich to do something about people travelling without paying. The ideas are shown with attractive flash short animations which all last about three seconds and show the point of the idea without words. You see a ticket machine, for example, which issues a bus ticket, then the ticket turns over and on the back of the ticket I see the sentence "collect 10 tickets and get a free Cola".

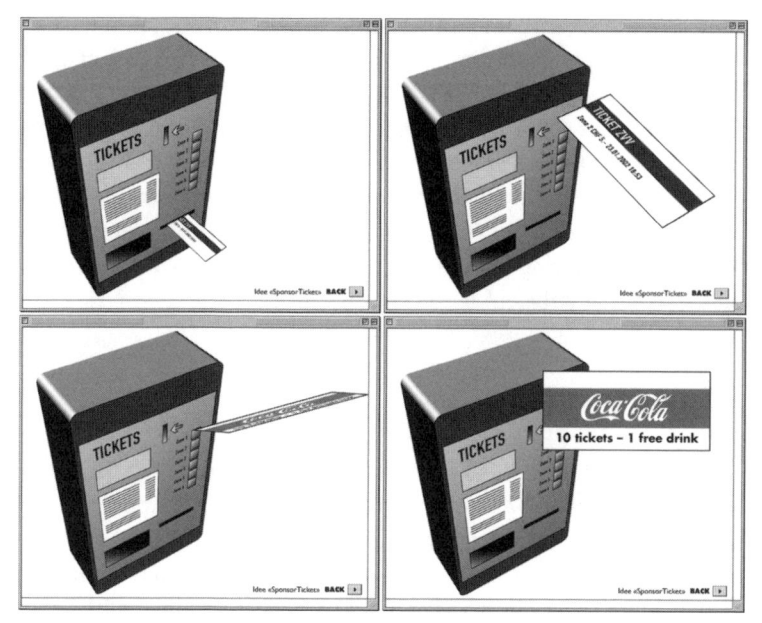

The idea "buy 10 tickets and get a free Cola" was shown using simple but effective flash animations.

The idea is clear immediately and I can categorize it and compare it with other ideas because they are all shown in the same form. Companies also like to present such ideas internally because the presentation form is so attractive and so simple. And, above all, the ideas can be passed on in this way without any loss of information. Otherwise it can happen that ideas become unfamiliar over time as a result of constantly explaining them to others, just like in the game "Chinese whispers", in which one person whispers something to the next person in the circle and so on, and by the time the sentence arrives at the last person, the original sentence is unrecognisable.

As soon as an idea is comparable, comprehensible and durable, the sender of the idea moves into the background, particularly when the suggestions of various people are presented in a uniform form. And that is exactly the purpose of IdeaDesign within the process of the industrial production of ideas. Even if you don't want to produce your idea industrially, you should take to heart the fact that various ideas are easier to understand and gain a structure if they are presented in the same form and a neutral person presents all the ideas. If you then carry out a disciplined selection procedure (see chapter "IdeaSelection"), the chance is considerably higher that you find the favourite idea (i.e. the idea which is most interesting and, at the same time, most widely accepted) more easily and quickly and therefore can start more rapidly with the implementation of your idea. This will give you a competitive advantage compared to your competitors who started thinking about ideas at the same time and presumably on very similar subjects as you.

SplitSecond

The advertising industry works on the principle that a poster or advertisement which is not understood within one second, doesn't work. The same thing applies to ideas. If the idea cannot be understood within a few seconds, then it won't work. For this reason, the visualisation must put the idea in a nutshell so simply that the core of the idea is understood immediately.

Disruptive details have no place in the presentation of an idea, because they distract from the core of the idea. For example, when we used a different coloured background for each idea in the idea presentation for a new salami product many years ago, the client said "I don't like the pink-coloured idea at all". The pink colour in the idea was of absolutely no importance, it was an unnecessary, distracting detail, which diverted the client's attention from the idea itself. The good presentation of an idea is a little like a caricature, an exaggerated representation of the idea, without mocking the idea.

Good visualisation is also a measurement of the quality of the idea: if no appropriate form of visualisation, no picture occurs to you for your idea, then the idea is often too complicated and needs to be reworked. If, on the other hand, various pictures of the idea occur to you and you can hardly make your mind up which is the best one to make the idea clear, then the idea has potential. Even ideas which at first sight are difficult or almost impossible to visualise, deserve the right IdeaDesign.

A good example is names. They are particularly difficult to visualise: the names can't be given a final design, because then they wouldn't be comparable. But if you simply present the names in their "raw form" as words, then the emotional component is clearly missing and that is essential as names are particularly emotional ideas. A little trick can be used here: the IdeaDesign for the new name of a large association of small electricians, for example, is presented to the clients on the vehicles the clients use – the clients can therefore immediately imagine the effect the name would have on their customers when used, even if it doesn't appear in the definitive future design. The presentation of the name in the form of an Internet page, an advertisement or in acoustic form, for example the telephonist who answers a call using the new company name, are suitable presentation means for the presentation of a name.

Subdued visualisation

Visualisation is the idea's servant; it needs to have a subdued and supportive effect and not dominate. That is also the reason why those responsible for visualising ideas need to place more value on the clear presentation of the idea than on their own "fame". The objective of idea visualisation is not to win a prize for best design, but to provide the clearest possible design. Self-presentation has as little place here as airs and graces. A good IdeaDesigner understands the idea which he is to visualise within a few seconds and can realise the briefing for the design in the way which is required of him. In an ideal situation, he can work with a number of visualisation styles and is, above all, quick.

We demand of the IdeaDesigners who work for BrainStore that they can realise an idea within one to three hours, depending on the complexity of the presentation style. We insist on speed because the total process of the industrial production of ideas can't take much time – our clients need to receive their idea within a clearly defined timeframe. The emphasis of the process is, of course, on the development of the idea itself and not on the visualisation. And yet, the visualisation must be as good as the idea itself.

A name can be shown very effectively on an object which is familiar to the receiver. A bus or a daily newspaper, for example, can present a name in a much better way than any other form of visual presentation.

The visualisation briefing

In the same way that the quality of an idea depends on the quality of the briefing (see chapter "Briefing & KickOff), the quality of the IdeaDesign depends strongly on the clarity of the visualisation briefing – as well as on the quality of the ideas and the skills of the Idea Designer of course. The briefing must include the picture worlds which are desired and the required style of the visualisation. How should the ideas be presented, what style would be correct? Don't take this decision too lightly, the decision depends essentially on the client: which style is most appropriate to the client? Is it a conservative company or a progressive one? Will the idea be implemented relatively quickly (which makes a realistic presentation necessary) or are you at first only concerned with studies or visions (which permits a pointed representation)? Are they complex ideas which are best shown by an illustration, or ideas which need a mix of photo-realistic presentation and illustration, because they are embedded in a particular real life situation? There are a large number of possibilities of coming to the point of an idea visually. When you select a style, it's best to follow the principle "as little as possible – as much as necessary".

Less is more

At the beginning of our activities as idea producers, we were convinced that our ideas should be presented in complex and, above all, lengthy concepts. So we gave our clients thick folders with complex derivations, strategic concepts and hundreds of illustrations and always before the actual presentation of the ideas, because we believed that our clients would like to occupy themselves with the background material and our concepts before our presentation. Unfortunately that wasn't the case and our clients were so bored by these massive tomes, that they were often no longer interested in the core of the matter, the idea itself. The result was that many ideas of which we are convinced today that they were really good and should have been implemented, were not pursued.

Today, we do exactly the opposite. We present our core ideas to our clients in a short, sharp and client-friendly presentation. The presentation of each individual idea takes one minute at most. Each idea is visualised in a meaningful way and the same visualisation style is used for each idea.

This strategy has proved to be exactly what's wanted. Our clients now concentrate on the ideas and on the contents, not on the form or the sender. The satisfaction rate of our clients and the implementation rate of the ideas increased substantially as a result – quite simply because the ideas could now also be presented with more conviction internally.

IdeaDesigner

Not any old designer can become an IdeaDesigner. In addition to many excellent designers, there are also those graphic designers who want to express themselves, i.e. they want to demonstrate their skills or their design fantasies in every picture. Good IdeaDesigners on the other hand, see themselves as real visualisers who explain ideas. A lot of them are among BrainStore's IdeaDesigners. They are real professionals in their specialist area, in industrial design, illustration, caricature, prototyping or flash animation for example. The really good ones amongst them have a company of various styles, can adapt quickly to various situations and put their own preferences or artistic ambitions in the background.

We can also use such visualisers to accompany the idea generation process and they like to get their hands dirty every now and again and join in wherever necessary. They document the idea generation process with their digital camera, sketch the participants initial ideas or help us with the briefing and the training of other IdeaDesigners, for example. All of them are quick and productive and therefore ideal partners for the process of the industrial production of ideas.

The IdeaDesigners are also members of our CreatingCommunity just like the participants in the idea generation process and are, therefore, simply components in the entire process. No more, but also no less. Designers and graphic designers who are used to having a completely free hand when designing, first need to get used to our way of working. They need to learn that they bring a service for a total result and are not responsible for the result. Normally it's the other way around: usually designers in particular, are expected to have a high level of input on content, probably because everyone knows that they contribute a lot to the contents.

Not all designers can cope with this challenge well. One extreme example was a small graphic design office with whom we visualised an idea for a campaign for panty liners aimed at girls. The idea generation process had been completed and we had a perfectly clear vision of the design of our idea, a simple ad in a youth magazine. We briefed the graphic design office who had a lot of fun with the task. The ad was perfect after two or three corrections and we showed it to the client who loved it. It's difficult to say exactly what the client loved: the idea? The graphics? Or the visualisation style chosen? The graphic design office was of the opinion that it was definitely their contribution which had made the client so enthusiastic – and immediately demanded to be paid royalties on the ads which were placed. Although the situation was perfectly clear and the graphic design office was clearly our contractor in the project and not the originator, the owners insisted on an appropriate payment for their copyright. That's the way the industry works and in many situations this interpretation is legitimate and also makes sense, because it protects the originators from arbitrary actions of clients and partners.

BrainStore works differently. The unlimited right of use for the ideas belongs clearly to the client. The copyright belongs to all those who take part. And these have been appropriately remunerated for their participation. As industrial producers of ideas, we take on a commission and develop an idea which is appropriate for the client with a variety of people from various perspectives. Everyone who takes part is an important partner and component in the process, and certainly an originator of the idea. In the industrial idea generation process moreover, it is completely irrelevant to think about who brought in which idea. An IdeaDesigner brings his expertise, his specialist knowledge and a special talent in a certain function of the process of the industrial generation of ideas.

Fortunately we had made a clear agreement in advance with our graphic design office on payment for the project and could therefore solve the issue simply.

The right visualisation form for each problem

Each idea has its own right IdeaDesign form. And the simplest form is often the right one. Simple ideas can be best visualised with simple means. But there are always exceptions to the rule: in some projects you need to be very creative to generate enthusiasm for an idea. That is particularly true for ideas which you know will strongly polarise the audience. In that case the IdeaDesign can be provocative.

For the Swiss railway restaurant car company (which no longer exists in that form) we developed ideas a few years ago on how the catering in the restaurant and the mini-bar could be changed. The CEO at the time was an open and innovative person, his team less so. We knew that we would have to tread a fine line, because we would need to satisfy both the expectation of the progressive boss and the reserved attitude of his team. We therefore decided on demonstration as the presentation form to visualise the ideas.

One idea, for example, was the "coffee man", a friendly young man who walks through the train in the mornings with a coffee tank and a tray and sells one product only: really good coffee. The idea was simple but we needed to show it in a clever, slightly exaggerated demonstration. We put Simon, one of our employees, into a silver costume, with "coffee man" emblazoned on his chest (a kind of parody on Superman) fastened a thermos flask transformed into a rucksack on his back and a tray with beakers, cream and sugar on his stomach. We added a tube to the thermos flask so that Simon could fill the beakers easily and directly. On my signal, Simon appeared in the presentation room and poured all of the clients a cup of fresh, hot coffee to their individual taste. The clients were delighted and, above all, they could imagine the idea much better in this way than if it had "just" been sketched. The "coffee man" had just proved that it is perfectly possible to serve coffee easily and quickly in a train.

Demonstration must, however, be used carefully as a presentation method, because it creates the impression that the idea is already in the implementation phase when in fact there are still a lot of open questions. This technique is, however, highly suitable for sceptical audiences. To exaggerate, you could say that if you present the ideas in a known environment, you make them part of the audience's daily life.

We developed some ideas for new yoghurts for the Geneva-based milk processing company Nutrifrais, which, amongst other things, produces and sells Danone yoghurts. One of around 15 suggestions was, for example, the "Happy Pack", a pack made up of 4 yoghurt pots filled with things which bring a small piece of happiness to life: strawberry yoghurt, a chocolate dessert, jelly-babies and a chocolate brownie.

We showed all products in genuine Nutrifrais yoghurt pots and produced a basic design for the pot and the lid for each product. We printed them on photo paper, to create an effect as close as possible to "real" yoghurts. Then we had to think about how we could best present the various product ideas. Our IdeaDesigner Sven had a simple but effective suggestion: we would present the ideas in a supermarket refrigerator for yoghurt. So we set about making a replica of such a refrigerator, including the appropriate lighting.

During the presentation, our clients behaved like consumers in a supermarket and searched around in the products for that which they noticed first. The pack was taken out and then explained by us with a short presentation until all packs had disappeared from the refrigerator.

The advantage of such a visualisation is that a new idea is embedded in a known environment. That is particularly important for visionary ideas. We developed ideas for new functions for coffee machine for the manufacturer of the machine. In the IdeaDesign, we were very tempted to embed the new functions (for example, using only one single knob to operate the machine) in a new form of the coffee machine. However, this would have been confusing, because we weren't concerned here with a completely new design for coffee machines, simply with new functions. The client was much more prepared to accept a crazy function if it was presented in the type of coffee machines currently used.

It was much easier for our client to understand the amazing idea of the "coffee machine with one-knob-operation" if he could recognise his familiar coffee machine.

A further presentation method which is very popular both with us and with our clients is animated flash presentation. Flash is a useful tool for demonstrating animated graphics and is used everywhere in the Internet nowadays. It can, of course, also be used outside the Internet. Flash bring static ideas to life.

One example of this, is the idea which we developed for a travel agency which wanted to know how it could have a presence outside of the travel agency in a way which would get attention, yet be inexpensive. One suggestion was a travel agency on wheels which could be taken to different places and have enough space for a computer station, leaflets, a display with the current last-minute offers, general promotional material and a flag with the travel agency's logo. In the Flash presentation, we first showed the closed trolley with one of the travel agency's salespeople standing by it. By clicking on the various areas of the trolley, doors could be opened and the above-mentioned tools such as computer, leaflets, etc. appeared. The final picture was the fully opened mobile travel agency. We visualised the other ideas in the same way and the ideas immediately began to come alive.

The long-term favourites in IdeaDesign are certainly illustrations and sketches, both made by hand and computer-supported. A two-dimensional design is usually sufficient to present an idea visually. The rule is: the more abstract and technical the idea, the more important it is to include an emotional component.

We developed ideas for new drinks packaging for SIG Combibloc, a manufacturer of drink cartons. These were shown in sober, technical computer drawings. The whole thing seemed harsh. Our solu-

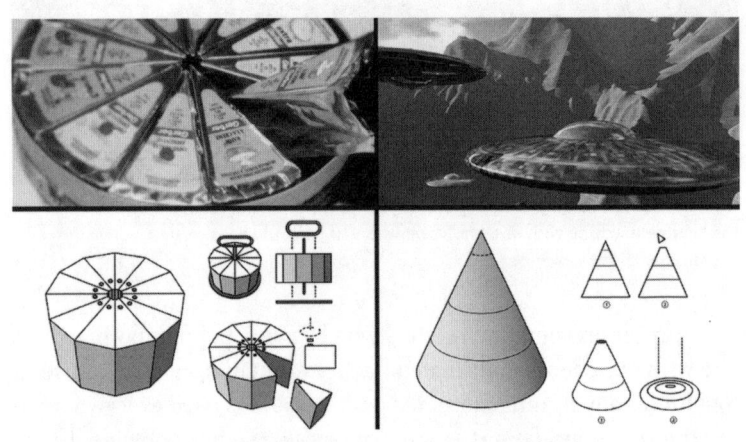

Mixing recognisable pictures with technical drawings can be used very well for representing new product forms. Visuals are Property of SIG Combibloc.

IdeaDesign

tion was to place a colour picture of the role model for our idea next to the technical drawing. For example, a UFO was the model for the idea of making drink cartons which can be squashed into very flat, UFO-like figures when empty. Or the picture of a pack of cheese spread triangles to represent a new, space-saving form for small packs (for coffee cream, for example).

Texts for good ideas

The visual presentation of the idea is not the only important thing, but also the language form in which it is presented. We have already explained that this should be short and attractive. It also needs to be written in a language which suits the idea. If, for example, we're talking about a technical product, then a sober, direct language is needed, for a communications idea for a new perfume a more flowery style would be appropriate. The usual rule applies also to the language presentation: less is more. The main purpose of the language is to say the essential things about the idea, to make it clear quickly what it is about.

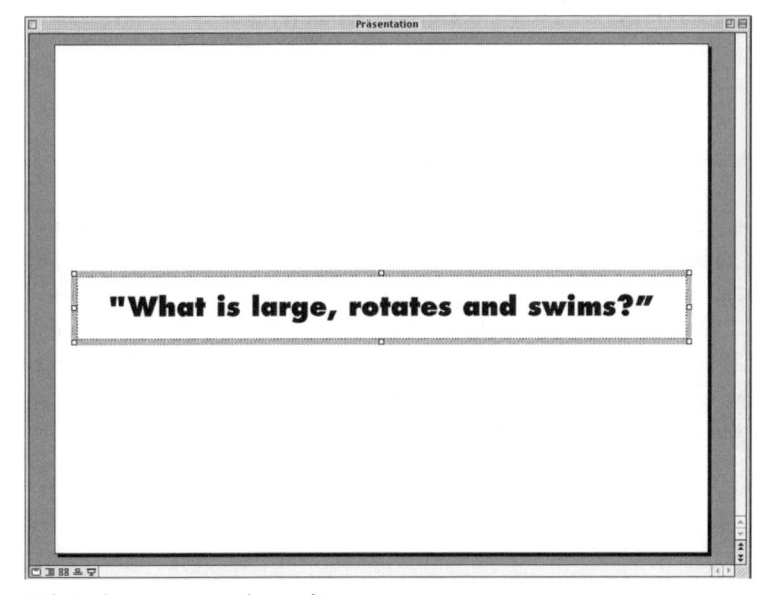

"What is large, rotates and swims?"

If you decide to make a presentation using PowerPoint, then there is a simple recipe, which ensures success:

Each idea is prefaced by a short teaser. This makes the audience curious about what is to come.

Page 1: A short "teaser" which briefly touches the subject of the idea, but nothing more. This page serves to help the audience distance itself from the introduction or the previous idea and be ready for the next idea. This awakens a certain expectancy and curiosity for the nest presentation.

Page 2: The idea is explained here. The visual presentation of the idea takes up the largest part of the page. You have 3 lines underneath in which you can briefly explain the idea.

Page 3: Additional explanatory details on the idea can be made here if necessary, information on implementation, things which have already been clarified, possible obstacles or role models from other industry sectors. If this kind of information is either unnecessary or not available, then you can do without this page.

There are few important rules for working with PowerPoint:

- Everything which has nothing to do with the idea has no place in the presentation.
- Avoid using decorative, brightly-coloured backgrounds, too many typefaces and font sizes.
- Define a master slide with all necessary typefaces, font sizes and your company logo.
- Do not use any other additional visual elements other than your idea visualisation.

The rules which apply in journalism also apply to describing ideas: use simple language with short sentences. Avoid foreign words. Address your audience directly. Explain the subject clearly and avoid unclear, fuzzy terminology.

The actual idea is explained using a visual presentation and a short description.

If you additionally describe your idea as a concept on paper, the following rules will be helpful:

- Use the same system as in the presentation: Teaser, explanation of the idea with visual support, further information if necessary. Ideally, you should also need a maximum of 3 A4 sheets per idea.
- Divide your text into short paragraphs, with a maximum of 3 lines per paragraph.
- Chose a pleasant font size and a common, discreet typeface.
- Use an index for quick reference.
- Avoid superfluous information and elements which don't help comprehension of the idea.

Alternatives to PowerPoint

Nowadays, PowerPoint is the most common tool for creating presentations. As useful as this tool is, it can be completely wrong to use this style for certain ideas. A PowerPoint presentation carries the risk of boring the audience with a presentation form they are used to and sending them to sleep. This places a fair evaluation of the idea at risk. Other possible presentation forms could be:

- Posters: A poster is designed for each idea which contains the same elements as a PowerPoint presentation. This gives you the opportunity of making the visual presentation of the idea much bigger than in a computer presentation. Hang the posters up in the room and make a guided tour from one poster to the next.
- Exhibition: If you work with 3D objects, you can make an exhibition of the ideas. The presentation objects are shown distributed throughout the room and a presenter for each object presents and describes it. It is important that you brief the presenters exactly on how they need to present each object, in order that they can be compared.
- Show or demonstration: A show or demonstration can be considered as a presentation form if the idea is very complex or the audience very demanding. This method requires a lot of effort and can only be justified if the idea cannot be presented in any other way in order to make them comprehensible to the audience. A show or demonstration is also a suitable tool to present ideas to a wider audience.

Core Concepts "IdeaDesign"

- Good IdeaDesign will make your ideas easy to understand, comparable and durable.
- Formulate a clear briefing for the presentation of your ideas and look for a suitable designer who can realise this briefing.
- Select the most simple presentation method (preferably illustration/sketch), unless the complexity of the ideas require another method.
- Where possible, include the IdeaDesigners in the process of idea development. As experts for example.

IdeaSelection

*The selection of ideas
is not a beauty contest*

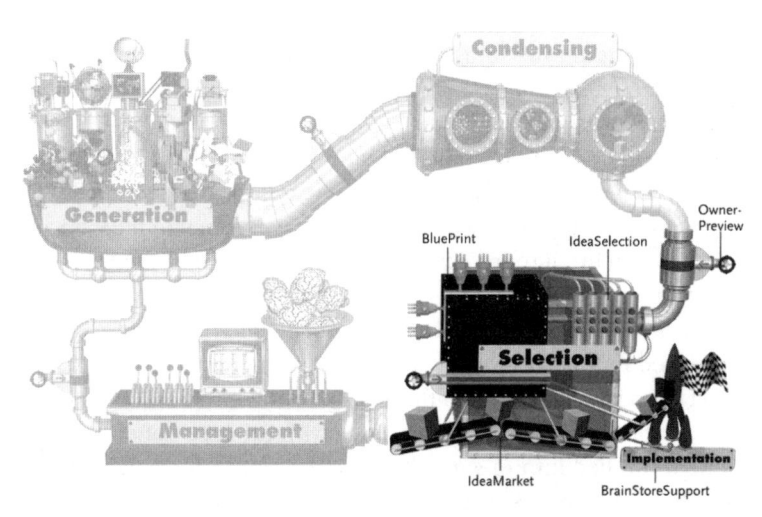

IdeaSelection is an important milestone in the development of ideas and helps you and the decision makers to select the best ides for implementation.

There's no question about it: ideas are a highly emotional matter, connected with positive and negative feelings. Unfortunately, every person has different feelings towards each idea. An idea which I personally find really great is possibly considered to be extremely bad by my colleague. And because emotions are non-negotiable, the positions will be immobile very quickly. This makes the selection of ideas extremely difficult. Even as an idea factory, we had to learn the hard way before we had found a method which actually allowed us to permit emotions in the evaluation of ideas, whilst keeping the decision process itself as unemotional as possible. For a long time, we found it very difficult to understand why the emotions boil over to such an extent in the final presentation of the ideas and why it is so difficult for our clients to agree on one or more ideas. We just noticed that ideas which had been developed in several phases and had been rated as good and interesting by our clients were often shot down at the presentation on the next decision level. Ideas which had been systematically developed in several phases suddenly disappeared into thin air, although various people from within the company had been included in the decision process and everyone was convinced of the potential of the idea. Ideas are simply something very fleeting; at first someone maybe thinks: wow, that's fantastic, and the second time, when he's perhaps in a different mood, he thinks: what's supposed to be so good about that?

It was very demanding, and I'm sure that you will have also experienced something similar yourself. It's just the same for our clients. In a name search project which she had managed without us, one of our clients in the agronomics industry had suggested 2 names to the management, which had overcome the obstacle of trade mark protection issues and were really new names which had never before been used in the agronomics industry. The names additionally met the criteria which a brand in this company must fulfil. The Director immediately rejected both names, one with the explanation that the name reminded him of something unpleasant in his personal life, the other with the reason that there was a chocolate brand with a very similar name. Both reasons were both irrelevant and very personal, which underlines the emotions which are always involved where ideas are concerned. Why did the director judge the name so personally? Why couldn't he assess it in a neutral and constructive way? Simply because he hadn't been involved beforehand and had no tools in order to be able to make his judgement in an unemotional way.

After analysing a number of projects, we established that two factors have a positive effect on the support given to the ideas at the end of the project:

1. The inclusion of decision makers at critical interfaces of the project. Decision makers who have been included feel responsible for the result, understand how the idea was developed and are more prepared to make decision in the selection of ideas.
2. A disciplined selection procedure for the idea. If the selection is made in a process which is structured and largely free of emo-

tions, then all the ideas can be examined with a healthy distanced attitude; the chance that an idea is rejected, which only awakens bad emotions in one person are lower.

We have constantly increased this inclusion and, whenever possible, we try to include the highest possible decision making level in the process. That doesn't mean that our clients need to accompany the entire process and have a lot of work with it; just the opposite; by being involved at the key points and decision stages, they don't waste any valuable time.

It was a little trickier to find a disciplined selection process which works. Whenever you present ideas, the emotions usually start to boil and everyone wants to have his say and air his opinions. The challenges for the selection process are extremely varied in a number of aspects:

- The right people must be considered in the selection of ideas
- The selection process mustn't be boring or appear bureaucratic but, at the same time, must proceed in a disciplined way.
- Everyone must keep to the rules in order that the ideas can be evaluated (which is not easy in an emotionally charged atmosphere).
- The results of the evaluation must be made available as quickly as possible, at best during the meeting.

Today we use a very cleverly devised evaluation process, which our clients understand, accept and regularly praise. You'll see yourself: as soon as you start to discuss and evaluate ideas in this way, then you will be able to implement many more ideas than before.

Preparation: material

In order to carry out an IdeaSelection, you need to have completed the stage "IdeaDesign", that means all of your ideas should be available in the form of a presentation and each idea should be visualised in some form. Whenever possible, you should discuss the entire presentation with your client, the ProjectOwner, before the IdeaSelection and ensure that the presentation is agreed by him and adapted to the language of the participants in the IdeaSelection. Take his input seriously, he knows his team better than anyone else.

Number the ideas consecutively in the presentation and in all documentation and label both the presentation and all of the participants' documents with the relevant idea number. Between 9 and 15 ideas is the ideal number. More than 30 is difficult, because the number is simply too large for the evaluation.

You will also need the following for the IdeaSelection:

- An overview of all ideas on a sheet of paper or on a presentation slide (again, don't forget the number of the idea).
- An evaluation form for each participant for each idea. The participants can make the following entries for each idea on the evaluation form:
    1. An evaluation, on a scale from 1 to 10, of how much he liked the idea.
    2. General remarks.
    3. Remarks on implementation / ability to be implemented.
- A form for preparing a rating list. All ideas are noted on the form, given a number and possibly pictured.
- An assessment programme in which the results of the evaluation and the rating list can be entered during the IdeaSelection. The most simple suitable tool is Excel, experts can also use a database solution, for example our BrainBase solution.
- The programme must be able to do the following:
    1. Calculate the mean value of the evaluations.
    2. Calculate the standard deviation (polarity) of the evaluations, i.e. show how strongly the opinions in the evaluations deviate from each other.
    3. Show the consolidated rating list of all participants, in which each one is given a position and then show them with the reverse value (the idea with the lowest value is at position 1).
- A beamer, with which you can show the results immediately.
- Writing materials for all participants.

When you carry out an IdeaSelection for the first time, it is important to test the whole procedure and your software thoroughly

– something we still do today before every presentation, to be certain that everything really does work. Nothing is more embarrassing than technical problems during the presentation of ideas. The whole thing is difficult enough without such unpleasant surprises.

In addition to the material you have available, you also need an assistant for the IdeaSelection, who helps you to collect the evaluations of the participants and enter them into the evaluation system. The IdeaDirector presents the ideas, the ProjectManager looks after the administrative side of things and the IdeaManager is there to answer any questions. (More on the roles in an idea project in the chapter "IdeaManagement").

Preparation: Invitation

The most important thing is not how many people take part in an IdeaSelection, but rather who takes part. You should nevertheless ensure that at least five people are present, because the statistical presentation of the results is somewhat meaningless otherwise. It is possible to carry out an IdeaSelection with up to 200 people, but you then need a lot of helpers for the entry of the results, or you won't be able to make the results known directly after the evaluation, although that, of course, is also a possibility. The advantage of having the evaluation directly at the beginning is that it can be demonstrated to the participants in an astounding way that their evaluation of the ideas does not necessarily correspond to the evaluation of the other participants, which significantly dampens the emotional components of the idea assessment.

When inviting the people who you would like to have present in the IdeaSelection, make sure that you have an optimum mix of competence and knowledge. It is also vital to include the decision makers in the process, as these are the people who will ultimately decide which idea is implemented. The people from the company should come from different levels of the hierarchy if possible, but have a loose connection to the subject of the idea generation. It is also meaningful to invite those participants who were already part of the idea generation process (see chapter "CreativeTeam") to the IdeaSelection. The inclusion of recognised experts in the project subject is also obviously helpful. These can usually be found within the company itself.

Inform the participants in advance of what they can expect at the IdeaSelection, in a letter or by email, for example.

Dear Mr. Steffen,

I am pleased to learn that you are prepared to take part in the IdeaSelection of the project "new chocolate products" on February 15th 2004. Please arrive at 9.50 a.m. in the conference room "Praline", in order that we can start punctually at 10.00 a.m. with the evaluation of the ideas. The meeting will last until 12.00 noon.

The objective of the IdeaSelection is to receive a wide feedback from decision makers and employees to our 15 new product ideas. You have been invited in your function as Marketing Manager.

The agenda of the meeting is as follows:

1. Welcome and short introduction
2. How the ideas were developed
3. Presentation of each idea; evaluation of each idea on an evaluation form (emotional evaluation)
4. Setting up of a ranking list of the ideas (objective, comparative evaluation)
5. Presentation of the results and the ranking list
6. Discussion/requests

The primary objective is not to agree on a product during the meeting, but to learn about the advantages and disadvantages of the ideas which we can then take into consideration in our analysis.

We look forward to seeing you and would like to thank you for your support at this important stage in the development of a new chocolate product.

Yours Faithfully

Rita Furtwaengler, Project Management

On the day of the IdeaSelection, you should arrive at the meeting room early and ensure that all logistical issues are working. Does your assessment programme function? Is the beamer properly connected? Is all necessary material available?

Carrying out the IdeaSelection. Welcome and introduction

At the beginning of the IdeaSelection you should make a short introduction in which you explain the purpose of the IdeaSelection and explain the rules.

The following points should be made clear:

- IdeaSelection is a structured process in which various ideas are presented and evaluated from different perspectives by various people.
- IdeaSelection is not a beauty contest. The objective is not to choose the idea which everyone likes best as the winner, but the one which clearly has the most potential.
- IdeaSelection is not a democratic process: the opinion of every participant is important and valuable, but the decision on which idea will ultimately be implemented lies with the decision makers.
- Polarising ideas are particularly interesting in the IdeaSelection process, meaning ideas which create a lot of disagreement: some of the participants find the idea very good, some of them find it bad. Such ideas usually prove to be particularly interesting in the market, because they create controversy and give people something to talk about. Not everyone thinks that such ideas are good, but those who find them good are particularly enthusiastic about them. There is a fantastic story which illustrates this fact. In 1963, the advertising agency BBD presented the tagline "We try harder" to the US company AVIS. The slogan was created for strategic reasons: AVIS is "only" the number two in the market. It needs to try harder to keep customers. The statement was then shortened to "We work harder" or "We try harder". The agency had surveyed customers on the slogan and found out that around 50 percent

found the message "We try harder" simply brilliant and remarked that it made AVIS appear to be a particularly credible company. The other 50 percent found the message ridiculous and said they would rather have a company which actually is better and is not just trying to be better. A clear and rather blatant polarisation. The agency therefore recommended to AVIS that they use another tagline. Robert C. Townsend, the CEO of AVIS became famous in the advertising world for his calm response to these results and this recommendation. He said: "I don't have a problem with 50 percent market share". The tagline is still used by AVIS today.

- It is important for the success of the project that everyone keeps exactly to the rules. Ask all participants to follow your instructions exactly.
- Explain the exact procedure of the IdeaSelection:
  – In the first round, the ideas are evaluated by the participants in secret. At this point in time the ideas shouldn't be discussed. The spontaneous, unfiltered opinion of each individual participant is particularly important in this phase. In this phase you also have no possibility of comparing the individual ideas – just evaluate each idea based on your "gut feeling". There is no such thing as a second first impression, that's why this stage is so important.
  – Make notes – if you wish – on each idea, either general remarks or comments on its ability to be implemented.
  – In the second part of the IdeaSelection, you will be able to see all ideas again in an overview. Based on this overview you will put the ideas into a ranking list, in which you put the ideas into a clear sequence, from the idea which you think has the greatest potential (number 1) to the idea which you think has the least or no potential for implementation. This evaluation should no longer take place based purely on emotions, but according to more objective criteria. Which idea can you imagine being implemented and which less so? Personal viewpoints will, of course, also be included, but, in contrast to the first evaluation, they should no longer be the centre of attention.
- Give the participants the chance to ask questions on the process and explain the individual steps again if necessary. Now you are ready to carry out the IdeaSelection.

If you think this procedure sounds pedantic and reminds you a little of your primary school teacher, then you're probably right. But experience has shown us in over 350 projects that nothing can be left to chance in the IdeaSelection stage. Nowadays, I even remain calm if we're carrying out a parallel IdeaSelection with participants in several locations, who can link in via a telephone conference. But only because I know that I have a formula for the evaluation of ideas, which functions across language, convention and cultural barriers. A participant from Latin America who was taking part in an IdeaSelection for the name for an agricultural product, took the time recently to send me an email in which he thanked me for having managed to "persuade their hard Latin American heads to take part in a disciplined evaluation process". Nevertheless, it is always clear to me when carrying out this stage, how fragile the balance is between disciplined evaluation and the underlying emotions and hierarchies.

Carrying out the IdeaSelection: Evaluation

Now we get to work. Present your first idea to a highly critical audience. That can really make you nervous, especially when you get an immediate and direct feedback from all participants in the room.

Present the idea calmly and as objectively as possible. If you have prepared the idea well according to the "IdeaDesign" stage, then this shouldn't be a problem. After each idea, give the participants a short amount of time to assess the idea on their evaluation form and make any remarks which occur to them. Make sure that you make neither too much nor too little time available. For me, the time to continue is when only a few participants are still writing. Ask the participants to complain themselves if they don't have enough time. Have your assistants collect the sheets immediately and enter them into the evaluation system. This rhythm usually works well after three ideas. Don't interrupt the idea presentation and don't take a break. As you are keeping the ideas brief, a presentation and the initial evaluation shouldn't take more than 40 minutes for 20 ideas.

Afterwards, you can ask your participants to each make one comment publicly at this point. Make it clear that you are particularly looking for the participants' expert knowledge at this time and that they should make a comment which is relevant for the next step, the preparation of a ranking list. Make a note of all these comments and then briefly summarise the comments, so that the participants can check if you have understood everything correctly.

Carrying out the IdeaSelection: Ranking list

The next step is the preparation of a ranking list of all ideas. This step is once again, carried out by each participant on his own. To do this, they need an overview of all ideas (number, idea description, possibly an illustration) and the ranking list form. Ask the participants to now put the ideas into a clear sequence, i.e. to give each idea a number. The clarity of the ranking list is so important because it cannot be evaluated otherwise. The task is either fairly easy or rather tricky, depending on how many ideas you have to evaluate. With more than 15 ideas it really isn't that easy to make a clear ranking, as the ideas don't differ from each other as strongly. Collect the completed lists and have them entered into the system. You will now presumably need a few minutes to enter the results, so you can take a short break again.

Carrying out the IdeaSelection: Presenting the results

During the break you will have entered all the results and have looked at them quickly in your assessment system. You should now be able to show three diagrams:

1. The mean value of all evaluations from the first round (presentation of all ideas).
2. The polarisation of the evaluations (formula: standard deviation).
3. The ranking list of the ideas.

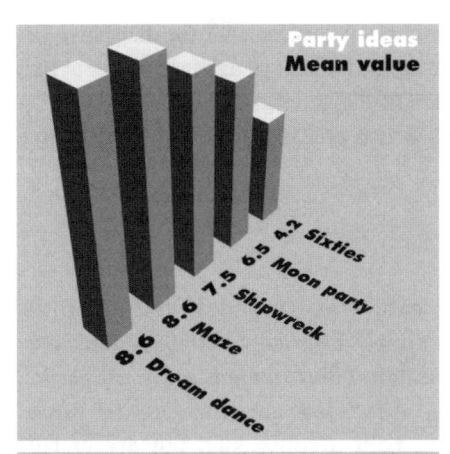

Carrying out the IdeaSelection: Presenting the results

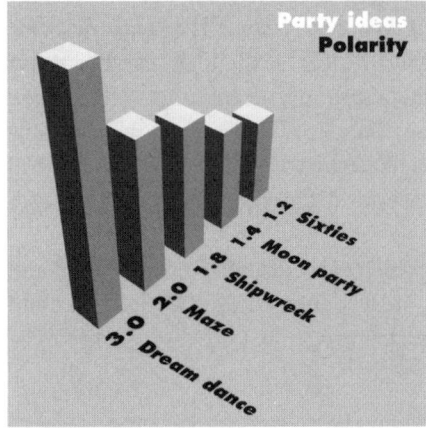

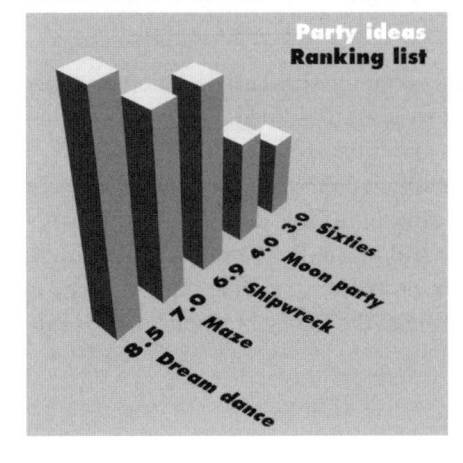

You should now present and briefly explain all three diagrams, i.e. show the current status of the ideas. Make it clear that this is not a final result, but an initial picture of the general mood.

There are a few comments which are basically valid for the three diagrams:

Mean value diagram:

- It often happens that the least provocative ideas end up on the highest positions. That is simply because such ideas don't normally have a strong polarisation effect, meaning that all participants can usually agree that these ideas are candidates for implementation. Such ideas can gain a consensus, but are usually colourless because of their low polarisation. I always describe such ideas as excellent "Plan B" ideas: if the team can't or won't agree on an idea which has a stronger polarisation effect, then such ideas can be an option. This is, of course, not what usually happens. There are often brilliant ideas, which get first place and where the clients ask themselves "Why didn't we come up with that ourselves?".
- Polarising ideas, i.e. ideas which some people find very good and some people find very bad, are also interesting. The disagreement on these ideas is usually much stronger and the discussion can be very interesting.

Polarisation diagram:

- Polarisation is nothing other than the standard deviation from the mean values which have just been presented. Every polarisation above 3 points is very high and interesting for the discussion.
- There are, of course, ideas which don't polarise at all or not very significantly; this either means that a large number of participants found the idea very goods and that it got a high position in the ranking list for this reason, or that most people think the idea is bad and it is therefore on one of the lowest positions in the ranking list.

Ranking list diagram:

- When looking at the ranking list, the most important thing is the comparison with the initial evaluation; it becomes visible here, how ideas have developed for the participants from the initial evaluation to the preparation of the ranking list, therefore how they have "grown on them". Those ideas are particularly interesting which were evaluated as poor or medium in the initial evaluation and suddenly appear at a higher position in the ranking list. The opposite also applies: ideas which were very positively evaluated in the initial evaluation and suddenly appear at a lower level in the ranking list. What are the reasons behind this change of mind? The participants can comment directly on this. This up and down is nothing unusual, particularly for highly emotional ideas such as a new name for a product. Names in particular, constantly develop and awaken new feelings every time they are looked at.
- If the participants have been appropriately instructed, the ranking list should reflect the potential of the ideas more than the personal preferences of the participants. Therefore, compare the ranking list with the initial evaluation from this point of view also.

After you have presented all three diagrams, ask each participant to pick out his three favourites and to explain the reasons for his choice. Then close the meeting and advise that an evaluation and recommendation – based also on the written comments – will be available in a few days.

Assessment and recommendation

Take the time to study all facts, comments and input of the IdeaSelection again in peace and derive a recommendation from them as to which ideas your client should implement. You can include less popular ideas in the final selection if you have the feeling as a result of the discussion and evaluation that one such an idea has potential, and if you can provide reasons for your recommendation. Trust the figures from the assessment, but don't trust them blindly. As the person responsible for the project, you should also trust your gut feeling and recommend those ideas, where you have the feeling after the entire project, that they should be implemented.

> **Core Concepts "IdeaSelection"**
>
> - In order to select the right ideas for implementation, a structured evaluation process should be used, to which you should invite all relevant decision makers.
> - The process of the selection consists of three steps: a) the evaluation of every idea on a scale from 1 to 10, b) the preparation of a ranking list, c) the selection of three favourites.
> - The evaluation is done anonymously; the various positions can therefore be compared on a neutral basis in the discussion.
> - The results of the selection process are analysed and condensed into a recommendation. The decision maker can now make his decision based on the available data.
> - IdeaSelection is neither a beauty contest nor a democratic process; its only objective is to provide optimum support for the selection of the ideas.

IdeaManagement

How to keep track of everything in an idea project

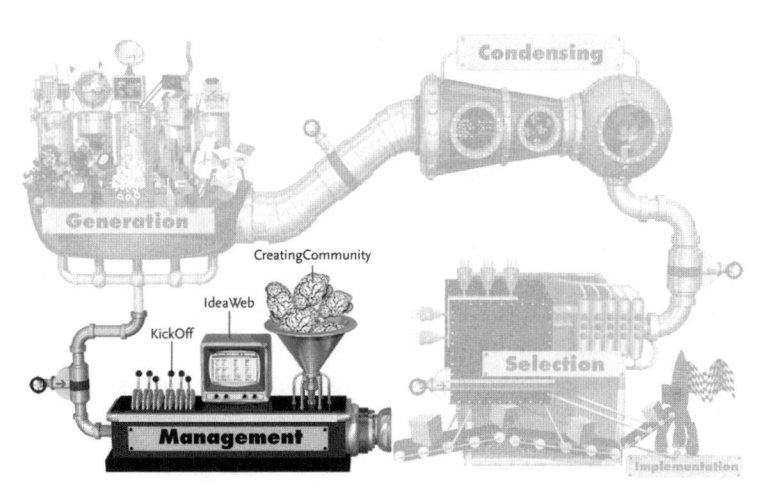

IdeaManagement ensures the optimum content and time related development of your idea project. You define, organise and enable a smooth procedure with the right people and tools – the end result is ideas which can be implemented.

Most people who apply for a job with us write in their application that they would like to work for us because they have a lot of ideas and believe that they can contribute these ideas in the best way in our team. Every single one of them is very disappointed at first, when they hear that the most important thing about a job in an idea factory is not contributing your own ideas, but coordinating and enabling other people's ideas. People who have a lot of ideas themselves are much more use to us as freelancers. What we need in our core team are people who see their strengths in enabling, preparing and structuring the idea generation process – a rare species, for at first sight, it is much more difficult to make a process available than to develop ideas yourself.

To be honest, we at BrainStore are extremely pleased that we don't have to create ideas ourselves every day, but can draw in suitable people from the CreatingCommunity for each project. From that point of view, the job of a producer of ideas is above all a management job: it revolves around knowing when who should be involved, how and when, in order that good ideas are developed.

That doesn't, of course, mean that our employees are boring and work only systematically. Their task is to ensure that, our clients are in possession of ideas at the end of an idea generation project which they can and want to implement. They don't have to be ideas which we really like ourselves, or which we can use to enhance our reputation. They have to be ideas which work. Such ideas are developed in a team where the participants treat each other with respect and curiosity.

In every project, we are very keen to see which ideas the process will come up with. At the beginning, we sometimes have a vague idea of the direction in which the ideas could develop and also discuss these ideas. Then we immediately let go of these images and just manage the process. I'm surprised every time how interesting, surprising and useful the ideas are. The process constantly brings up possibilities we would never have thought of ourselves.

A colourful mix

Although the idea producers themselves are "only" responsible for the process, we still need an interesting inspirational atmosphere at BrainStore. Through their presence, our employees must be in a position to bring our clients and every member of the CreatingComunity quickly to the point which is necessary for a productive workshop. And for that, we certainly don't need nondescript kind of people – they need to be interesting, inspirational and sharp.

The people who work for us are a mix of highly varied people. In the 14-year history of BrainStore, the mix of salaried employees has been and is very heterogeneous. Their fascination for our process, crystal clear analytical thinking, wide general knowledge or a particularly unusual perspective is more important than education and specialist knowledge. People with a résumé which is very straight lined and impressively consistent, which is what is wanted in most companies, don't have much of a chance with us: more important for us, is what someone has seen in his life, what he has experienced and achieved, than whether he or she knows everything about a specific subject. To a certain extent, we are all "Brains" - as we call each other at BrainStore – autodidacts. Unfortunately, you can't yet learn the profession "industrial idea producer" at a school or in a university education. Someone, for example, who leaves school at 17, but can already use language perfectly and was the leader of a Boy Scout groups for many years, is much more interesting for us than a business studies graduate who has never even had a summer job.

The willingness to fit into this team of idea pioneers – and we still feel like pioneers – and find a place there, is important to us. Other important characteristics are being able to withstand stress, take criticism and speed; furthermore a completely natural ability in working with computers, perfect use of language, excellent knowledge of at least one foreign language and, most important, commonsense.

Over the years, we have had a wide variety of people, both with and without a school or university education. Below is a small selection of the more than 80 people who have already worked for BrainStore:

- René, who left school at 17 and writes brilliant texts. Four years at BrainStore, today Creative Director of the advertising agency TANK in Estonia.
- Pascal, an 18-year old with a high school leaving exam, a cynic and thinker. Two years at BrainStore, today a student.
- Daniel, psychologist and co-founder of a Montessori school. Two years at BrainStore, today the Director of a Montessori school again.
- Sara, high school leaving exam. Two years at BrainStore, today a television newsreader.
- Pinck, hyperactive teenager with fantastic ideas and innumerable projects. Three years at BrainStore, today lives in California where he is, amongst other things, a helicopter traffic reporter and the assistant of a university professor.
- Risa, Swiss-Korean with iron discipline and an analytical mind. Today, a film-maker.

- Doris, former confectioner. Four years at BrainStore, today bookkeeper at Switzerland's largest advertising and communication school.
- Toth, longhaired heavy metal rocker. Two years at BrainStore, today Biel's fastest cycle courier.
- Thilo, skater and skateboarder. Two years at BrainStore, today a fundraiser for the WWF.
- Nora, who did a commercial traineeship with us and says the most friendly "Good morning" you have ever heard. Today training to become a nurse.
- Urs a sign writer and Sabine a trainee in a Swiss tank factory. Two years at BrainStore, today they have their own advertising agency.
- Sven, a brilliant designer with a weakness for military objects and a great love of ducks. Today a graphic designer and teacher at a design school.
- Saori, an 18-year old Japanese girl, who managed to make 13 appointments for BrainStore with the heads of the largest companies in Japan within the space of two weeks.
- Petra, cosmopolitan Swiss woman with perfect English and perfect manners. Today studying for her doctorate at Columbia University.
- Nicolet, wild kid, one year at BrainStore, today stylist for the presenters at the TV channel Viva Switzerland.
- Mägi, former project manager for the WWF. Today lives in London and works for a well-known market research institute.
- And currently: Sandro former hotelier; Anna, former fashion designer; Meesha, former artist, Barbara, former car sales person; Jan, brilliant web programmer and Jan, brilliant IT person; Markus, broke off his degree course; Laurent, spoiled genius, Pascal, former fashion retail salesperson; Martine, former owner of a hemp shop, Cornelia, former businesswoman and Japan expert; Sam, works part time at BrainStore and part time for the Swiss government, Kate, former hairdresser; Pia, education junkie; and Lea, office cat. We also have our own kindergarten, called Mini-Brains, which is attended by eight children.

All in all, that seems like a fairly crazy group of people, no question about it. Nevertheless we are the kind of people who are enthusiastic about the opportunities and the possibilities offered by the industrial production of ideas and who try to get more out of this system every day – for our clients.

Our Brains are particularly enthusiastic about the variety of our clients and commissions. Every day is an adventure or, as Sandro, our production manager says, "There's no way anyone here could say they've learned nothing today". And it's true: in a BrainStore career you acquire colourful but also deep knowledge from a wide variety of industry sectors, which also makes our employees attractive for other employers.

No period of grace – what IdeaManagers need to be able to do

If you want to build up a strong team in your company, which can produce ideas industrially, then you need people who can start to contribute from day one. They need to be people who like to jump into cold water and would rather have too much to do than too little. They also need to have a good feeling for the show aspect of a project. For an idea generation project is also a stage production in many parts, in which everything has to function to the minute. Make sure you take on people who get things done and who can also think, not the other way around. Thinking can be trained, doing can't.

A good way of putting together a management team for an idea project, is an assessment with all applicants. Don't be afraid to put pressure on the applicants. Here is a selection of exercises which we carry out with potential Brains to test their ability as IdeaManagers.

- **General knowledge.** Do the applicants have a broad base of general knowledge (for example, can they name all current Ministers, assign a date to an event, and explain a biological term)? Can they logically categorise sizes and units (do they know, for example, how much a litre of milk currently costs, a kilo of gold or a Porsche Cayenne S)?
- **Association test:** What occurs to the applicants when they hear terms which are really only known to insiders? Which images and events do they think of when certain words are mentioned?

- **Idea evaluation:** Which ideas do the applicants select from a BrainStore pre-selection? And what reasons do they give for their selection?
- **Teamwork:** How do the applicants work in a team? How do they organise themselves? Who takes the initiative, who becomes the leader? Who thinks in a structured way?
- **Abstraction ability:** How quickly can the applicants understand a long, complex text and summarise it in three sentences?
- **Language ability:** How well do the applicants express themselves in German, English and a further foreign language? Can they formulate? How good is their spelling and grammar?
- **Dealing with clients:** How do the applicants react to telephone calls? How do they deal with clients who come to reception? How well can they improvise?
- **Technical skills:** How good are the applicants' computer skills, can they tidy up a filing system, work systematically, set priorities?

All of these indicators are important for the selection of your team. But what's even more important, is that the chemistry works within your idea team. IdeaManagers have to work closely together and need to be able to work smoothly and well together even in difficult situations. In our team, that is usually more of a challenge than project stress or tight delivery deadlines. For this reason, we as the company's founders don't present the team with just anyone we think is good as an IdeaManager, but try to include the whole team in the decision where ever possible (with 20 people that's just about possible).

Division of roles in the IdeaTeam

Ideas are a highly emotional issue. You can't keep ideas "at a distance". As soon as you start to work with ideas, you either like them or you don't. Yet distance is a decisive component for the success of an idea generation project. On the one hand, it needs people who are closely involved in the process and play a role in shaping them; but on the other hand, other people are needed who observe the project from a distance to guarantee the quality of the ideas. This division of influence is important, there is otherwise a risk that everyone is too strongly involved and surrounded by ideas to such an extent that they can no longer judge if an idea is really worthwhile or not.

For this reason, there are always two people in our projects who are responsible for the clients: an IdeaDirector and a ProjectManager. The IdeaDirector is in charge of the project. He holds the meetings and negotiations with the client and is responsible for presenting the ideas at the end of the project and recommending one or more ideas to the client for implementation. The ProjectManager accompanies the client through the project and is closely involved in the project. He looks after the client during the joint workshops, makes interim reports or takes up questions from the client, which he then discusses with the IdeaDirector. The ProjectManager supervises the production of the project and works closely with the responsible people in the IdeaProduction. Together with production, he also selects those ideas which are to be put forward and presents these ideas to the IdeaDirector. The IdeaDirector for his part, doesn't actively take part in the production process, but controls the quality of the ideas at clearly defined stages and evaluates whether the ideas meet the client's requirements. This system of "checks and balances" has proved its validity in hundreds of projects.

For you and your IdeaTeam, this means that you need to structure your project teams in such a way that one person is responsible for the success of the projects and keeps out of the idea whirlpool and maintains an overview of what is going on.

The core of the idea production is also a two-man team: the PeopleManager and the IdeaManager. They are responsible for carrying out the client's commission. The IdeaManager plans the project with regard to the content and time-related process, the PeopleManager provides the necessary resources from the CreatingCommunity. These two factors of time and people are the first and most important factors in an industrial idea generation project and are planned first.

People and timing

Who should be involved in the project and when? This question is discussed in a meeting of the core team, consisting of The IdeaDirector, the ProjectManager, the IdeaManager and the PeopleManager. Special wishes on behalf of the client or the project management flow into the planning. This meeting can, of course, only take place when the client's commission is clear (see chapter "Briefing & Kick-Off). We make the timing for the project binding in order that the idea machine can be reliably adjusted. It happens only very rarely that we deviate from a defined time schedule as this brings our whole machine and the entire network to a standstill and that costs money. As soon as the time schedule is clear, the required profile of the CreatingCommunity participants who are to be involved in the project is discussed. This profile is then published by the PeopleManager in suitable channels such as our website or advertisements, in order that suitable people can apply to participate. The size of the team and the type of experts who are included in the project is guided strictly by the idea generation project's budget. The optimisation principle also plays a role here. If the budget is very limited, in terms of either money or time, then less people and less expensive experts are used. If we have a generous time and resources budget, then we can plan to include larger teams and more expensive experts.

Once the project team has been found, the actual idea production process, which is subdivided into the phases of generating ideas, condensing ideas and selecting ideas, can begin. In the first phase we set the tools *CreativeTeam, IdeaInterviews and ExpertInterviews, TrendScouting and NetScouting*. In the second phase, it's the turn of *IdeaCity, FirstScan, CriteriaScan, ThinkTank and IdeaDesign*. The ideas are subsequently evaluated and selected in the *IdeaSelection* and then move on to *Implementation*. The detailed question of which tools are to be used, and how, depends on the client's briefing and the budget. The exact sequence of the tools, for example, if certain production stages are carried out in parallel, is a question of the time schedule. A short business project at BrainStore lasts two days from the date on which we receive the commission, costs 13,750 euros and involves 30 people in total. A large project lasts four months, is carried out in three countries in parallel, involves more than 2,000 people and costs 395,600 euros.

The path through the project

Once the tools and the people have been determined, the detailed planning of the individual production stages can begin. There are clearly defined preparation tasks for each stage.

- **KickOff:** The ProjectManager finds out all there is to know about the client's company and provides an overview of the most important facts and figures. A list of questions on the project is prepared together with the IdeaDirector. After the KickOff with the client, the ProjectManager formulates the briefing and organises a kick-off meeting with everyone who needs to be informed.
- **CreatingCommunity:** The project team discusses which skills are important in the current project and how the team of freelancers should be put together for each stage. The PeopleManager publishes the various jobs in suitable channels, filters and analyses the applications, holds castings and assessments and then suggests the selection of people to the project team. After that, these people from the CreatingCommunity are called in and briefed. The PeopleManager also ensures that there are no gaps in the documentation of the people who will be used and organises the whole complicated administration of these contacts, meaning payment of their fees and travel expenses, social payments, address management and feedback.
- **CreativeTeam:** A detailed program for the development of idea components must be prepared based on the client briefing, the logistical side of things also needs to be planned and the rooms prepared. The database in which the raw ideas are entered must be prepared and all participants must be cast and briefed for the event. The performance team, which will become the CreativeTeam, meets in preparation meetings and tests the entire programme in a dry run to find out if the desired results can be achieved with it, or whether changes need to be made.

- **IdeaInterviews and ExpertInterviews:** If this tool is used, then a survey concept needs to be prepared, a sample of the people to be questioned needs to be defined and a questionnaire developed. Preparatory tasks are also necessary in this stage, such as the provision of the survey database, the testing of the questionnaire with 5 percent of the sample and the briefing and casting of the freelancers who will carry out the survey. Contact must be made to the interviewees, appointments made and survey documentation prepared (for example, demonstration material). When the survey results arrive, they must be entered by the interviewers and checked by the IdeaManager. The results are finally evaluated and documented in a results paper.
- **TrendScouting and NetScouting:** A detailed briefing is written for the TrendScouts or NetScouts, which states what they should look for in their region. Logistical questions, such as flights or possibilities for sending the material which has been found, need to be clarified and the database needs to be prepared for entering the results. Once all the material has arrived, then it needs to be sorted, classified, entered in the database and evaluated.
- **IdeaScan.** All the ideas from the generation phase need to be entered and clearly documented. They are then prepared in various forms for the IdeaScan and made available to the participants. Ideas which are formulated in the IdeaScan have pictures added where necessary and are edited by the IdeaManager so that they can be worked on in the next phase.
- **ThinkTank:** Moderation of the ThinkTank is the responsibility of the IdeaManager. He needs to have the task and criteria framework in his head, know the background of the project by heart and lead the ThinkTank team.

    The most important thing is the systematic evaluation of the existing ideas and their continuous refinement. During the ThinkTank with experts, the IdeaManager carries out the research necessary to confirm that there are no doubts that the ideas can be implemented.
- **IdeaDesign:** The IdeaManager prepares the briefing for the IdeaDesigner and discusses it with the IdeaDirector. After that he asks for quotations and samples of work from various designers and then signs a contract with the person most suitable for the job. Parallel to IdeaDesign, the ideas are formulated in a presentation.

- **IdeaSelection:** The IdeaManager prepares the presentation and the test documentation for all ideas. Every idea is printed on a small card in order to make it easier for the participants in the IdeaSelection to prepare a ranking list. A database has to be set up and programmed for the entry of all evaluations and comments.

The project team also accompanies the client in the implementation stage, sets up contacts to possible partners for the realisation, leads meetings at project milestones and coordinates the various people and organisations involved in the implementation if required by the client.

Idea clients need a lot of love

The preparation and the control of the process are not the only challenges for the IdeaManagement, looking after the people who commission the ideas, i.e. the client is also demanding and of central importance for the success of the project. Buying ideas is not a routine purchase. We invest a lot to develop informal and strongly service-oriented dealings with our clients. It is very important to us hat the clients understand how the ideas are developed and where their involvement is decisive to success.

Don't forget that in our projects, our clients come up against a situation which is completely new for them. It starts the moment they enter our idea factory, which is a completely different environment to that which employees of companies are generally used to. Then, in the CreativeTeam, they work together with outsiders, who are often several decades younger than them; the mere prospect of this can trigger a high degree of nervousness, and there are many clients who ask us before the workshop how they should behave, what they should wear and what they should generally be aware of. The project management must foresee such questions and provide the right information, but without deflating the surprise effect on the day of the CreativeTeam; the fact that worlds collide here is one of the major advantages of the industrial generation of ideas including outsiders.

Perfect appearance is part of customer care. Ideas and the process of the industrial production of ideas are already experimental enough, the clients doesn't need to experience other surprises. We make every effort in our documentation and in our correspondence with the clients to create an impression of clarity, brevity and, above all, a uniform, unmistakable appearance. It is important to us that people who entrust us with their idea projects are aware that they are dealing with professionals and that their project is in good hands. That obviously doesn't mean that we never make a mistake or that everything is always perfect; but is important to us that we strive for perfection and we surpass the desired quality in almost all cases.

If you decide to set up IdeaManagement in your company, modelled on the industrial production of ideas, then you will do so because you are convinced of some of the elements of the idea machine. You need, however, to be aware that not all of the employees in your company will be of the same opinion and will have absolutely no understanding of the controlled chaos, which the inclusion of outsiders for example, brings with it. You can best confront this (hopefully only initial) scepticism if you are well organised and professional and look after your internal clients in the project perfectly. A clear division of tasks will help you in this. You don't have to do it in exactly the same way that we do – there are a thousand other possibilities. But take a look at our procedures and decide which ones could work for you. The division of tasks in IdeaManagement which is described here has proven its validity.

Quality assurance

The evaluation of the quality of ideas is a demanding task and keeps the IdeaManagement occupied throughout the entire process. We are not prepared to pass ideas which develop in the industrial generation of ideas process on to our clients without a quality check. A quality control check takes place at every new stage of the project. My partner, Markus Mettler always compares this to the task of a good Head Chef: he also always wants to be sure that the dishes which leave his kitchen are perfect, that's why he stands at the door and looks at the works of art very closely, tastes here and there and thus guarantees that only perfect creations leave his kitchen. The

Head Chef also relies on a good, smooth process in his team, but he still does the final check himself.

In an idea generation process, the IdeaDirector takes on this role. He guarantees towards the client that the quality of the ideas is faultless. There are two checks necessary for this: firstly, the ideas must correspond to the client's briefing. If, for example, the implementation of an idea is not supposed to cost more than 300,000 euros, then it is simply unprofessional if we present ideas which would cost 700,000 euros, however good they may be. Or if the requirement is that the idea can be implemented and supervised by a team of two people, then it makes absolutely no sense to present ideas where an entire football team would be needed to implement them. The IdeaDirector rejects such ideas in the name of the client. The second check is provided by BrainStore's internal criteria: Is the idea really simple? Is it surprising for the client? And how relevant is it? Any ideas which do not pass this test land in the wastepaper basket.

Debriefing – learning from mistakes for the next project

You can improve things in every idea project. You can and must learn from these things in order to adapt the process to the increasing requirements. The process shouldn't develop into a dogma, the tools mustn't start to rust. The idea machine must be regularly maintained and developed further. We do this very pragmatically on the one hand, by preparing an analysis after every stage with the team responsible for that stage in the project. We start with the positive aspects: what worked well, what was fun, what did we like? Every member of the team writes down at least three points, then we exchange them. There are a lot of positive things to say every time, which confirms to us and the participants that the process works and that we can rely on it.

Then, the negative aspects are collected. Here again, everyone writes down between one and three points. Each point is discussed and analysed. The IdeaDirector collects the points and comments on them where necessary. Each point is also written down. Points which keep coming up and are looked at closely by the production team:

what can we change, what can be improved? The last item in the debriefing is tips and practical advice: every participant makes a note of at least one tip on how the process could be made to work even better next time.

Sometime these are extremely simple suggestions for improvement which we can directly implement in the next project and sometimes they are suggestions which cannot be implemented in the short-term, but are added to our list of necessary developments (for example, an adjustment to the software or a change to the room layout).

These debriefings are of enormous help to us in constantly optimising the idea generation process and keeping it alive. We do, of course, also listen to our clients and ask them what we could improve in the process. What we get from clients is usually more general remarks from which we can measure satisfaction or dissatisfaction with a specific subject, rather than pragmatic advice on the idea generation process as. These images of the general impression are also integrated into the short-term or medium-term improvements list.

Core Concepts "IdeaManagement"

- Your "client", meaning the person or department who commissioned the idea, is your yardstick for the quality of the ideas: orientate yourself fully to his wishes and requirements, which you have developed with him in the briefing (see chapter "Briefing & Kick-Off").
- Tackle an idea project in twos if possible, by allocating one person to look after the client and accompany the project from a certain distance (IdeaDirector / ProjectManager) and one person to take on the role of IdeaManager / PeopleManager. If the budget for the idea permits, then break down the division of roles even further. This makes particular sense in complicated projects.
- Your task as IdeaDirector / ProjectManager is to explain the process to your clients, to accompany them through the process and ensure the quality of the ideas.
- Your main task as IdeaManager / PeopleManager is to prepare the project and to plan, to get the right people from your CreatingCommunity on board and to ensure that good ideas result using the right tools.

- If you want to include further people in your IdeaTeam (for example, if you have to manage several projects in parallel), make sure you take on people who act rather than people who think. People who can always keep the process going and who are fascinated by idea production. Pay attention to speed, a feeling for language, abstraction ability and broad general knowledge, and, above all, make sure that the chemistry in the team is right.
- Determine the time schedule and the profile of the people who you want to involve in the project right at the beginning and stick to it. Remember: the industrial production of ideas functions according to the optimisation principle, and keeping to the time schedule enables a concentrated, cost-conscious and result-oriented way of dealing with the subject matter "idea". You will have come up with an optimum result at the required point in time.
- Treat your clients, even if they are internal clients, with care, foresight and respect: they have commissioned an important good for the future of your company, an idea. Keep the balance between an informal atmosphere, which is necessary for the production of good ideas, and a certain distance, which is vital for providing optimum advice to your clients and, ultimately, for the recommendation of the idea to be implemented.
- If you are the client for an idea yourself, insist that your IdeaTeam keeps to a clear process in which at least the phases of generating, condensing and deciding on ideas are kept separate from each other. Don't get too involved in the project yourself but take a clear stand at key stages (Briefing, CreativeTeam, IdeaSelection) and bring the project onto the course you have set.

Implementation

How to implement ideas whose time has come

You are no doubt occupied with the implementation of ideas every day, and as someone who is predominantly occupied with the development of ideas and not the implementation of them, I wouldn't presume to give you advice on doing so. However, what I can certainly show is the connection between the systematic development of an idea and the systematic implementation.

Let's assume that you have developed an idea industrially by separating the phases of generating ideas, condensing ideas and making a decision, including the right insiders and outsiders, testing the idea and ensuring its acceptance at all levels of the company. If you have done all that, then the implementation itself is really child's play. All you need is a clear plan, the best possible people, a crystal clear time schedule and the necessary funds. It is important that you regard the implementation as the natural and logical continuation of the search for ideas and that you don't throw away the many methods, people and resources, which you have invested in the idea by having poor implementation.

I have, unfortunately, often experienced how an excellent idea has been spoiled beyond recognition by details and small changes which at first appear harmless. These changes are usually well-meant and are supposed to serve the idea, in fact however, they usually water the idea down and move it away from its amazing, simple core. This watering down generally already happens during the selection of the ideas (see chapter "IdeaSelection"). Decision makers who are too concerned with the achievement of a consensus tend to mix a number of ideas together. They take a little bit from each idea and mix them up into a new idea.

An example: as part of an election campaign, we developed tactical last-minute ideas for one of Switzerland's major political parties, ideas on how the party could pull undecided voters over to their side in the last few weeks before the election. There were two ideas which the party preferred: the first idea was an activity whereby the party members would distribute an information leaflet and a packet of Alka-Seltzer with the message "Don't risk a hangover after the elections" in public places shortly before the elections. The information leaflet would clearly refer to the party's middle-of-the-road position and make it clear to the voters that this party stood for pragmatic solutions and that therefore no-one needed to fear a hangover on the day after the elections. The idea clearly lived from the party members and their direct contact with the people. The second idea was pure communications, a poster with the headline "Four years is not a flirt". This campaign would also have been accompanied by an activity, in which party members would have directly addressed passers-by. In the end, the party leadership printed an advertisement in a few newspapers which showed an Alka-Seltzer and the slogan "A headache for four years?" and called upon people to go and vote. I wonder how many people were persuaded by this half-hearted campaign to vote for the party concerned. The mixing up of ideas brought nothing in this case. It only watered down the effect and, additionally, created little pressure by leaving out the active element (directly approaching people on the street). There are, of course, good examples for the mixing of various ideas, but this decision should be made out of real conviction and not purely to achieve a consensus.

The mixing of ideas is only one way of poorly implementing ideas. Another possibility is to keep changing apparently small details. In this way, a completely simple idea can turn into an confused disaster in no time at all. Another example from the world of communication illustrates the point:

When we created the product "Track 7" for the Swiss Railways, SBB, a youth railcard with which 16 to 26-year olds could use all trains in the Swiss railway network free of charge after 7 p.m. for a small annual charge, SBB commissioned their usual advertising agency, a globally recognised, international advertising temple with the communication of the product to the target group. The product's message was extremely simple: "Travel free on the trains after 7 p.m." The young people we had questioned in a survey found the product and the basic idea very interesting. So the agency started work on making this product known to young people. One day I was walking along the street, when I suddenly saw a poster. I recognised immediately what it was about, namely, our product "Track 7", because I recognised the logo on the poster. What I seriously doubted however, was that the young people who were supposed to use "Track 7" would feel themselves addressed by the poster. The poster mentioned nothing about train travel, nothing about free of charge, nothing about 7 p.m. The message was completely different "Track 7 offers you so much that it doesn't even fit on this poster", together with a picture of a young person, who was obviously happy about something, and the logos of various companies, who appeared to have something to do with this happiness. What had happened? The advertising people (and presumably their clients) had thought it necessary to enrich the basic idea of the "Track 7" card with various additional benefits, special offers for young people, special prices for concerts and marketing offers for the target group, for example. There's nothing wrong with that. Presumably however, the new partners also wanted to be mentioned in the communication. This watered down the core idea "free travel after 7 p.m." and the new partners didn't even have any benefit from the communication. Bad luck for everyone. Thanks to the good and simple basic idea of the product which was developed together with young people and whose benefit spread quickly amongst the target group, "Track 7" was nevertheless a success.

The third possibility of badly designing the implementation of a good idea is poor information in the team. A poorly informed of employees base certainly won't communicate your idea well to the clients. The best concept is of no value when your employees don't know what you want to achieve with it. We experience exactly that effect as customers every day: attractive facades of companies behind which the employees at the sharp end have not been sufficiently informed about new strategies, behaviour or important information for the customers. Or, they have the information available, but haven't been given sufficient training to communicate this information. To invest in ideas and their implementation under these conditions is a waste of money when it comes down to it.

For everything you develop on the top floor, the question is: how can I communicate it to all employees? To do this, not surprisingly, you need a lot of new, good ideas again.

Only include the best

As opposed to idea development, where the rule "a lot of varied, less-qualified people rather than individual highly-qualified people" applies, the rule when it comes to implementation is "as many people as necessary, as few people as possible, and only the very best". The insights which are valid for the CreatingCommunity in the production of ideas, also apply in principle to the implementation: look for the most suitable people for the implementation by inviting proposals for the project from a wide variety of people and organisations. Give as many people or groups of people as possible the opportunity of getting to know the basics of the project and of offering a contribution to the implementation from their perspective. At BrainStore, we call this the "IdeaMarket"; it is an opportunity for people who could be involved in the implementation to get to know the project, to comment on it and then to offer their services. The project team for the idea, the clients and a handful of interested people, who could imagine taking part in the implementation of the idea are present. It goes without saying, of course, that everyone involved signs a confidentiality agreement and that the project management does not reveal all the facts at this stage. An IdeaMarket brings a lot because it doesn't work with fixed teams ("We'll do it with the company "Great Parties") but enable unusual combinations ("Great Parties can do the catering, because they are the best at it and Nice Place will be responsible for finding a suitable room, entertainment and the accompanying programme"). The IdeaMarket offers an immediate opportunity for questions, fine tuning and comments. You can't exclude the possibility that the idea will be given a final polish here. It really is worth getting the best people and groups on board for the implementation, the success of your idea is determined here.

BluePrint, your implementation concept

In order to prepare the implementation, you need not only a good team but also a watertight implementation concept, which is constantly adjusted during the project. This BluePrint, similar to the blueprints used in engineering, is nothing more than the idea paper developed in the ThinkTank, which is now enriched with exact implementation details, milestones and cost information.

A BluePrint is a rolling paper and contains the following information:

1. The detailed concept of the idea, with the who, what, how, when, where, why. As many details are included as possible. The sources of information should always be stated (for example, "Professor Meyer, from the ETH says that the object should not be larger than 3 x 5 cm, in order to fit into the machine 100045-E"). In this way, you always have the possibility of referring back to the source if something is not clear. It is also advisable to set up a database with all telephone numbers and email addresses of these sources.
2. Ongoing planning. We use the model "what is okay", "what is not okay" and "next steps/responsibilities". A very simple recipe admittedly, but one which has proved its worth. The ProjectManager of the project has the task of keeping this list up-to-date on a daily basis and also carrying out regular meetings with everyone involved in the implementation. Such meetings should take place no less frequently than every two weeks, in extreme cases, it may also be necessary to hold daily meetings.

The implementation team needs a clear division of roles and tasks. The shorter the time for implementation, the more important it will be to be able to rely on this division. The core team, consisting of client, IdeaDirector and ProjectManager also plays a decisive role here; they are the driving force in the implementation and can decisively influence the success of a project. You will also have to be prepared for bumpy roads in every project. I have never, really never experienced an implementation project in which everything went smoothly. Sandro Morghen, our production manager, remembers with horror what happened at the printers one day before Easter: the production of an important object for our client BMW was almost ready for print acceptance. The printer told us at the printing machine that he unfortunately didn't have a pantone colour scale (a colour palette with an exact allocation of colour tones) and had therefore mixed the colour (the typical BMW blue) "by hand". Changes could no longer be made, it was after all Easter. If you have production experience, then you can imagine our production manager's horror. Thanks to the diplomacy and eagle eyes of our production manager, the BMW blue was perfect in the end.

Sometimes the difficulties are on a small scale, sometimes they are real crises. In both cases, you need this strong three-man team to manoeuvre yourself out of the mess. If there are three of you then you have possibilities, can act and master the crisis. For example, in every project where something has to be produced (and that is usually the case), then there will be problems with the production. In a three-man team, one person can be there to supervise the production, one can look after the implementation team and one can look after the, probably nervous, stressed-out client. If you were alone, that wouldn't all be possible at the same time.

We have already implemented a lot of projects, from simple events, the design and print of several hundred thousand complex printed materials to demanding projects such as the production of plastic figures in China or the carrying out of several complicated training sessions for the employees of a multinational company. In many cases however, our clients implement the ideas themselves and don't involve us or only let us accompany the implementation. The latter involves coaching the client project teams with regular meetings and the continuation of our BluePrints. In this way, we can significantly increase the efficiency of our clients' implementation

Know what is important

According to my experience, the most important things in an implementation project are setting priorities and keeping a clear head. If you have the best people for the implementation at your side, then nothing can really go wrong regarding quality. It is important that you don't impair this quality through bad planning or the wrong decisions. Every person in the team has a clearly defined role, based on their expertise. Make sure these roles are clear at the beginning of the project and also make it clear that the project management role has the last word on time schedules and decisions. In this way you can control the project more easily and better. The inputs from experts are definitely wanted but the project management must think of the well-being of the project as a whole and therefore call a halt to suggestions from the people doing the implementation when it gets out of hand. I have often experienced, for example, that I need to make it clear to the implementation team, that the ideas already exist and "only" have to be implemented. New suggestions are wanted in the detail work, but are no longer of value in the larger concept. Be careful also with the inclusion of people in the implementation who do not speak the same language as your team. If you have hard realists in your team and let an emotional lateral thinker loose on these realists, don't be surprised if the attitudes harden. In the implementation phase, we're no longer concerned with fresh ideas, but with the concrete realisation.

Convince others of the implementation

The really hard work in implementation is not carrying it out effectively, but convincing the old hands in the company, that this idea really does have to be implemented. If you included the decision makers in the selection of the ideas, then you shouldn't find it difficult in the implementation phase to gradually gain the support of the remaining employees. Go step by step and, if necessary, convince people individually of the idea which needs to be implemented. Make these agreements in writing and make it perfectly clear that you expect a binding commitment here. Do not underestimate the effort involved in this process: you need the support of every single participant in order to be able to enforce an idea in your team. You will, of course, have to convince an entirely different team depending on whether you want to implement a small idea (for example, a client event) or something larger (for example, a new logo in connection with a completely new presence on the market). With larger projects, you will not only have to convince the management, but also make allies out of the whole workforce and inform them in great detail about the changes coming up.

A decisive point in the implementation of larger projects is the attention of your employees. You can direct attention in projects using various measures. Here are a few examples:

- **Repetition:** Constantly repeat the objectives of the project and the desired end result by using different methods, for example, screen savers, emails, information events, memos, updates of concepts.
- **Glamour:** Announce an "After Project Party" on the very first day of the implementation for example. Recruit a small team which is responsible for organising this party and constantly informs the team about facts concerning the party (where it will be held, who has been invited, who will speak, what there will be to eat, special activities etc.) In this way, everyone is motivated to keep at it until the concept has been realised.
- **Friendships/team spirit:** Friends always get special attention. You can, for example, define a "Mr. Project" in each team, who courts attention for the implementation project in a friendly manner in his team, discusses with others, shares ideas and reports on the general mood of the team etc.
- **Threats:** Threats are a method which needs to be used with care. It works extremely well, but it isn't always an acceptable way of getting attention nowadays: Slightly watered down forms are, for example, a project countdown in the entrance hall which every employee sees when he comes to work or regular reports on setbacks and successes.

Core Concepts "Implementation"

- Implementation is the logical continuation of idea generation. Decide on one or more suggestions and pursue their implementation unerringly. Make sure that the ideas don't become watered down by blending ideas with don't fit together or by constantly changing various details of the idea until the idea is no longer recognisable.
- Look for the best possible partner for the implementation either from within the team or outside of it. In this phase, you need genuine experts. But make sure that those responsible for the implementation are compatible with your team and create a common language and working platform.
- Make your team and the company's employees into allies for what you plan to do; if necessary, collect individual decision makers personally and record one-to-one the objectives which have been agreed in discussions with employees and objectives meetings. In large projects, make sure that even the very last employee communicates the idea at the front, i.e. with the customer.
- Plan the implementation pragmatically. Put together a project team of at least three people, who predominately look after the project. Record the progress of the project and open issues in regular meetings and inform the entire team (down to the base) about interim successes.
- Keep the attention of your team as high as possible in large projects, by drawing attention to the project in various ways using various methods and styles.

Parting words

*Brilliant ideas
can be organised*
Julius Robert Oppenheimer,
American physicist (1904 – 1967)

Dear readers, I hope that I have been able to make the world of the industrial generation of ideas a little more accessible to you. The constant development of the process and the tools for the systematic development of idea is our team's passion; I'm sure that there is still a lot to discover to make the process clearer, simpler and more structured for our clients and for ourselves. Our idea factory is still something new, we are still pioneers, yet we are convinced that service providers who, like BrainStore, work with a highly systematised process and put together the right participants for each question on an ad hoc basis, will gain in importance everywhere in the near future, and that companies which continue to develop their innovations in an unsystematic way will have to face major competitive disadvantages.

I hope that you can draw on our tool kit in your company or organisation and in your personal projects and have fun developing ideas with a system, quickly and with the right mix of people.

This book could only be written because many people made a contribution to it; first and foremost, the entire BrainStore team, who have helped to develop our process over the last 14 year and who give their utmost every day, then our clients, whom we have to thank for hundreds of exciting commissions and interesting questions. I would also like to thank:

- Markus, my husband, for his persistence, his humour, his criticism and for looking after our children on many, many weekends.
- Nemo and Ella, my children, for distracting me from writing, for their laughter, their curiosity and their questions.
- Oliver Gorus, my agent, for his pragmatic and constructive editorial work.

- Sven Weber, the book's illustrator, for the illustrations he created at triple speed as usual.
- The Swiss Railways (SBB) for a perfect railway network with electricity for my mobile office.
- Johanna and Wilfried, my parents, for their support and everything which they gave to me as I made my way in life.

Appendix

Further reading and Web links

We have had bad experiences with published Web links and literature references during our projects: you can never rely on the references being up to date. We want to be more innovative on this issue; at our Web address

http://www.brainstore.com/ideamachine/

an updated list of recommended reading and Web links is available which supplements this book. That also has the advantage that you only have to click on the Web address and not type it in.

As an additional benefit from the book, we also provide working materials for idea workshop at this Web address which you can download. Try it out!

The author

As co-founder and chairman of BrainStore AG (Biel, Switzerland), **Nadja Schnetzler** is a pioneer in the industrial production of ideas. BrainStore was founded in 1989 and has since developed into an international network of highly modern idea factories with an environment of over 2,500 freelancers who are organised in teams for the generation of ideas.

BrainStore developed a clever idea production process and a system of 16 freely-combinable basic processes which are continually developed further and have proved their value in hundreds of projects. In addition to the production of ideas on behalf of companies, BrainStore supports companies in setting up their own internal idea factories. Furthermore, idea workshops are carried out for individual people, teams and entire organisations. Leading knowledge and research institutes throughout the world, such as Cornell University, Geneva University or the IMD in Lausanne occupy themselves intensively with the BrainStore processes and teach their students the BrainStore methodology. BrainStore's list of clients includes companies of all sizes and from all industry sectors.

The illustrator

Sven Weber drew the illustrations in this book. He has been called the "King of Lego" since his early childhood and therefore became a graphic designer, although he actually thinks that advertising is superfluous. The part-time hypochondriac swears by mayonnaise and soft drinks which contain caffeine as an essential part of human nutrition; he would, however, never eat duck, due to his unlimited admiration for these animals because of their triple motor functions (waddling, swimming, flying). He considers the Apple Macintosh to be God's most perfect creation and hopes to achieve world dominance of this perfect being in the medium term. Once had an impressive collection of noble moral principles, most of which are, however, rubbish.

Index of persons

b
Bruckner, Anton 73
Burst, Laurent 65, 170

c
Curie, Marie 24

e
Einstein, Albert 23

g
Goethe, Johann Wolfgang von 23
Gogh, Vincent van 23

h
Hanks, Tom 21
Heche, Anne 22
Hoffmann, Dustin 22

l
Langenscheidt, Florian 10

m
Madonna 78
Mettler, Markus 178
Morghen, Sandro 187
Mozart, Wolfgang Amadeus 23

n
Nicollier, Claude 100
Niro, Robert de 22

o
Oppenheimer, Julius Robert 193

r
Renold, Ursula 57

t
Townsend, Robert C. 160

v
Vinci, Leonardo da 24

w
Weber, Max 11

Index of companies and brands

a
Apple Macintosh 197
AVIS 159 f.

b
BBD 159
BMW 67, 89, 104, 187 f.
Bosch 25
BrainStore 9, 15, 21, 30, 34, 36, 44, 47, 51, 55, 57, 60 f., 63–66, 68, 74 f., 79, 82, 90 f., 105, 111, 113, 117, 119, 122, 125, 130, 132, 135, 141, 144 f., 168 ff., 174, 179, 186, 193
History of 168
Career 58 ff., 65, 171
Business-School IMD 87, 196

c
C&A 62, 78, 93
Coca-Cola 34
Cornell University 196

d
Danone 146
Deutsche Bank 87
Dupont 25, 57, 70, 78

e
Economics Department of the Danish Government 41
Embraer 25, 77
essor 23

h
Häagen Dazs 130

i
IMD Lausanne 87, 196

j
Johnson & Johnson 35

k
KODAK 130

l
Logitech 25
Lycra 57

m
Mars Company 112
MediaMarkt 44
Migros 51, 78
MindLab, Copenhagen 41

n
NASA 22, 100
Neckermann 111
Nestlé 60, 80
Neue Zürcher Zeitung 36
Novartis 111, 129
Nutrifrais 146

p
PowerPoint 150 ff.

r
Rolex 125 ff.

s
Siemens 25
SIG Combibloc 78, 148
Syngenta 43, 76, 78
Swiss College of Communication and Marketing
(Schweizer Fachschule für Kommunikation und Marketing) 130

Swiss Federal Agency for Vocational Training and Technology (Schweizerisches Bundesamt für Berufsbildung und Technologie) 57

Swiss Ministry of Health (Schweizerisches Bundesamt für Gesundheit) 66

Swiss railway restaurant car company (Schweizerische Speisewagen Gesellschaft) 145

Swiss Railways (Schweizerische Bundesbahnen, SBB) 55, 98, 184, 194

u

University of Geneva 87

z

Zurich public transport operators (Verkehrsbetriebe Zürich) 138

Subject index

24-hour telephone hotline 119

a
Ability to be implemented 156, 160
Absolute rubbish ideas 129
Abstraction ability 172, 181
Acceptance 12, 26, 35, 183, 187
Addressing young target groups 55
Adrenalin level 91
Advertising agencies 26f, 66, 159, 169, 170, 184
Agricultural business 43
Airs and graces 141
Alternatives to PowerPoint 151
Ambitions, artistic 144
Analysis of the procedure 27
Ancillary criteria 45f, 54, 128, 131, 135
Appearance of interviewers 104
Architect 11
Assessment 24, 156 f., 159, 162, 165, 171
Assistant 157, 169
Association test 171
Associations 9, 80, 141
Assumptions 77, 101
Atmosphere 74 ff., 92, 94, 104, 107, 124, 155, 168, 181
Attention 86 f., 92, 105, 124 f., 138, 140, 148, 160, 189, 190 f.
Attitude, criticism-free 76 f.
Authority 34, 70 f.
Autodidacts 169

b
Background material 143
Background work 92
Bad 12, 50, 60, 96, 153, 155, 159, 164, 185, 188, 195
Base work 73

Basic mechanism for producing ideas 34
Basis 37, 41, 47, 68, 97, 101, 132, 166, 187, 193
Beamer 80, 156, 159
Beauty contest 153, 159, 166
Best practice 36
Binding commitment 189
Blueprint 186 f.
Brain 79, 122 f.
BrainBase 128, 130, 156
BrainCharting 89 f.
BrainRace 84 f.
BrainStation 82 f.
Brainstorming 9, 21, 23, 26 f., 47, 77, 79 f.
BrainWriting 81
Breaks 90, 92, 94, 134 f.
Briefing 27 f., 33, 39, 40, 42, 45–48, 50–54, 73 f., 90, 101, 114, 117, 124, 131, 133 ff., 141 f., 144, 152, 174 ff., 179 ff.
– for the IdeaDesigner 141
Bringing together insiders and Outsiders 34
Budget, levels 41
Burnout 13, 68 f.

c
Career 58 ff., 65, 171
Caricature 140, 144
Carrying out 119, 159, 161 f., 173, 187 ff.
Catering 92, 112, 145, 186
Changes 51 f., 54, 175, 183, 187, 189,
Changes to the briefing 51
Changing details 184, 191
Chaos 40, 61, 178
Chaos and structure 40
Cheeky 62
Chicago 76

Subject index | 203

Chief Innovation Officer   36
Children   9 f., 41, 45, 79, 86, 96 ff.,
    103, 118, 125, 170, 193
Chocolate brand   39, 154
Chocolate product   40, 52 f., 158
Cinema   115, 116, 123
City of ideas   123 f.
Client, internal   45
Client briefing   124, 133, 174 f., 179
Client portfolio   43
Coaching   68, 188
Coffee   48, 88, 92, 146 f., 149
Combiner   124, 126 f.
Commission
– formulating   47
– unclear   11
Commissions from private individuals
    47
Commonsense   25, 169
Companies
– innovative   14, 36
– technology-driven   26
Company culture   40 ff.
Company innovator   69
Compass for the idea generation project
    47
Competitive advantage/-disadvantage
    140, 193
Complaints   9, 96
Components of ideas   26, 35, 73, 98,
    124, 157, 175
Comprehensibility   138
Concept   37, 100 f., 104, 107, 151, 185 ff.,
    189, 190
Concepts   28, 33, 35, 37, 54, 72, 94, 107,
    120, 143, 152, 180, 190 f.
Condensing ideas   21, 28, 30, 37, 119,
    122 f., 127, 137, 174, 181, 183
Condensing   phase 33, 74, 94, 97, 118,
    138
Confidentiality   69, 72, 186
Contents   77, 119, 138, 143 f.
Conviction   143, 184
Coordination   32 f.
Copyright   145
Core idea   140, 143, 173, 185
Core team   13, 29, 72, 113, 167, 174, 187
Cost information   187

CreatingCommunity   29 f., 55, 61, 65,
    68, 72 f., 144, 168, 173 ff., 180
CreativeTeam   40, 51, 53, 73-78, 87 f.,
    90, 92-95, 97, 101, 110 f., 116, 125, 127,
    129, 157, 174 f., 177, 181
Creativity   15
Crises   188
Criteria, experts   128
CriteriaScan   31, 123, 128, 131 f., 174
Cross-references   118
Culture   14, 40 ff., 57, 60, 104, 112 f.,
    120
Cultures, different   43, 56
Curiosity   14, 61, 63 f., 97, 150, 168, 193

d
Daily grind   75
Data quantity   121 f.
Database   65, 105, 116, 118, 123 f., 127,
    130, 156, 175 ff., 187
Dealing with clients   76, 172
Debriefing   179 f.
Deciding on ideas   28, 181
Decision-makers   12, 22 f., 28, 32, 35,
    43, 50, 54, 62, 153 f., 157 ff., 166, 183,
    189, 191
Decisions
– attitude towards making   50
– makers   12, 22 f., 28, 32, 35, 43, 50,
    54, 62, 153 f., 157 ff., 166, 183, 189, 191
Demonstration   145 f., 152, 176
Describing ideas   150
Design, appropriate   117
Designers   52, 67, 70, 143 f., 176
Detailed knowledge, cumbersome   43
Detailed planning   175
Details, disruptive   140
Differentiation   36, 37, 58
Difficulties   21, 26, 44, 58 f., 64, 188
Direct   62, 93, 114, 149, 161, 184, 189
Discretion   69
Distance   44, 101, 150, 172, 180 f.
Division of tasks   178, 187
Download   195
Durability   138

e

Education   10, 57, 65, 99, 130, 168 f., 170
Edwin   130
Efficiency   24, 32, 68, 102, 135, 188
Efficient   13, 24, 37, 96, 122
Emotions   31, 130, 153 ff., 160 f.
Employees   12 ff., 24, 26, 30, 32, 36, 47, 51, 56, 61, 66, 87, 93, 96, 112 f., 116, 119, 127, 146, 158, 168, 171, 177 f., 185, 188 f., 191
Endurance test   31
Engineers   13 f., 22, 25, 61, 77, 97
English   66, 93, 117, 170, 172
Evaluating what already exists   102
Evaluation   15, 54, 97, 102 f., 105 ff., 119, 122, 130, 138, 152 f., 155-158, 160 f., 165 f., 172, 176, 178
– Sheets   161
– System   157, 161
Evaluation Statistical   106
Evaluation of surveys   105
Excel   105, 129, 156
Exceptional people/individuals   23, 105
Exchange   60, 95, 125, 179
Exercises   171
Exhibition   113, 116, 152
Experience, many years of   25
Expertise   145, 188
Experts
– retired   99
– discussions   30, 133
– interviews   35
– knowledge (specialist)   32, 70, 134, 145, 161, 168
External perspective   61, 69 ff.
Extreme positions   69

f

Factory atmosphere   74
Family-owned companies   13
Fascination   168
Favourite idea   14, 97, 138
Feasibility   31, 33, 128, 133, 135
Feat of strength   56
Feeling   14, 28, 43, 133, 153, 160, 165 f., 171, 181
Fees   175
Film   21 f., 67, 169

Finding business areas   119
Fine tuning   186
FirstScan   31, 123, 128 f., 131 f., 174
Flash
– animation   139, 144, 147
– short animations   138
– presentations   147 f.
Flexibility   68
Flipchart   27, 80, 91
Foreign languages   169, 172
Foreign words   78, 150
Form   27 f., 31, 52, 54, 72 f., 87, 103, 106, 118, 124, 130, 135, 137-143, 145, 147, 149, 152, 155 f., 158, 161 f.
Formulations, intellectual   78
Foundation   46, 73
Fountain of youth   62
Framework   10, 32, 39, 41, 57, 176
Freaks   99, 107, 120
Freelancers   67 f., 112, 117, 167, 175 f., 196
Fun   15, 62 ff., 75, 80, 85, 97, 99, 116, 144, 179, 193
Further development of a company   36
Further developments, marginal   58
Future idea producers   50

g

Garden   124
General knowledge   65, 168, 171, 181
Generate – condense – decide   26, 74, 181
Generating   ideas 11, 13, 26, 45, 91, 102, 174, 183
Generation phase   28 ff., 45, 97, 109, 121-124, 135, 176
Gold nugget   76
Graphic designer   27, 67, 117, 143 ff., 170, 197
Group of people, crazy   170
Group, homogenous   56, 58 f.
Gut feeling   160, 165

h

Hierarchies
– flat   36
– levels of   14, 70, 157
History of BrainStore   168
Hollywood   22, 67

Subject index | 205

i

IdeaBook 124
IdeaCity 30 f., 121, 123 ff., 127 f., 135, 174
IdeaDesign 31, 134 f., 137, 139-142, 145, 147 f., 152, 155, 161, 174, 176
IdeaDesigner 134, 141, 143, 145 f., 176
IdeaDirector 157, 173-176, 179 f., 187
IdeaInterview 40, 116
IdeaManagement 33, 157, 167, 177 f., 180
IdeaManager 118, 129, 133, 157, 172 ff., 176f, 180
Ideas
- polarizing 129 f., 159, 164
- three-dimensional 86
- uncomfortable 132
- visionary 80, 147
- brakes 60
- clients 154, 168, 177, 188
- condensing 21, 28, 30, 37, 119, 121 ff., 127, 137, 174, 181, 183
- descriptions 132
- evaluation of 138, 152 f., 157f, 161, 166, 172, 176, 178
- experts 128
- factory 23, 27, 29, 32 f., 35, 43 f., 110, 135, 153, 167, 177, 193
- filter 128, 133
- fragments 28, 30, 78, 122
- generation of 13 f., 21, 28 f., 36 f., 43, 56 f., 61, 145, 178, 193, 196
- generation phase 28 ff., 33, 45, 97, 109, 121-124, 130, 135, 176
- generation team 45
- machine 21, 25 f., 28, 31, 35 ff., 55, 97, 128, 132, 174, 178 f.
- management 32 f., 37, 39
- network 29
- paper 186
- parking space 45
- production, industrial 15, 25, 29, 32, 34-37, 79, 95, 102, 128, 139, 141, 144, 177, 178, 181, 196
- search, systematic 25, 61
- selection of 31 f., 154 f., 166, 183, 189
- team 118, 172

Ideas as the motor of the whole Company 36
IdeaScan 176
IdeaSelection 32, 97, 106, 140, 153, 155–163, 165 f., 174, 177
- parallel 161
IdeaTargets 26, 29, 95 f., 98
Identification 44
Illustration 124, 126 f., 142, 144, 152, 162, 194, 197
Illustrator 124
Implementation
- concept 186
- project 188, 190
- rate 143
- team 188 f.
Incentive 113
Inclusion
- of outsiders 14, 178
- of the ProjectOwner 31, 134 f.
- of young people 62, 87
- of decision-makers 154
Individual performance 12, 69
Industrial design 144
Industry sector knowledge 43
Information, loss of 139
Information, poor 185
Initial material 29
Initial situation 46, 54
Innovations Important 57
Incremental 110
- management 12, 14
- pressure to innovate 23
Inputs, international 118
Insider/outsider mix 34, 74
Insiders 34, 56, 61, 128, 171
- and outsiders 28, 29, 30, 34, 55, 61, 64, 68 f., 70, 72 ff., 89 ff., 94, 110, 124 f., 135, 183
Inspiration 11 f., 22, 24 f., 28 ff., 37, 54, 61, 74, 80, 82 f., 88, 94, 113
Interested parties 42
Interior design 77
Internal perspective 69, 71
International aspect 110
Internet 28, 65, 111, 117-120, 141, 147
Interviews 30, 35, 97, 104, 106 f., 110
Introduction 27, 150, 158 f.

206 | Subject index

Inventing 24
Inviting proposals 186

j
Job applications 167
Job opportunity 65
Journalism 150

k
KickOff 33, 39, 43, 45, 50, 54, 73, 90, 128, 142, 175
Kick-off meeting 43 f.
Killer expressions 59, 63, 128 f.
Kindergarten 10, 45, 170

l
Lack of interest of today' youth 63
Language ability 172
Language, common 44, 191
Lateral thinkers 67, 128
Laughter 91, 193
LavaLamping 31, 132
Limits 40
Location 43, 76
Loners 12
Luck 12, 185

m
Main criterion 45 f., 54, 128, 131, 135
Mainstream ideas 129
Management job 168
Manager 13, 22, 39, 44, 48, 51, 60, 64 f., 68, 71, 87, 110, 121, 125, 137, 158, 170 f., 187 f.
Managers 39, 41, 62 f., 65, 79, 87, 91, 97, 125, 172
Mantra 26
Map 39 f., 51
Market
– research 22, 35, 98, 123, 170
– survey 96
Marketing 24, 36 f., 44, 55 f., 58, 63 f., 71, 77, 119, 122, 130, 137 f., 158, 185
Marking the playing field 40
Material 24, 29, 43, 54, 57 f., 76, 78 f., 82, 86 f., 90, 92 ff., 116, 119 f., 124 f., 128, 143, 148, 155, 157, 159, 176
Matter of taste 31
Mean value 156, 162, 164

Meetings 64, 137, 173, 175, 177, 187 f., 191
Methodology, knowledge of 33
Milestones 177, 187
Minute-taker 81
Misunderstandings 42, 120
Mix, colourful 168
Mixing of ideas 184
Mobile phone technology 26
Moderation 34, 134, 176
Moderator 78 f., 81, 83 f., 94, 124, 132 f., 135
Monastery 22
Multiple choice 103
Museum 48, 123
Music, inspirational 82

n
Name for a new car 27
Name-finding project 78
Native language 93
Needle in a haystack 12, 40, 121
Needs of the target group 101
Network of freelancers 67
Network, systematic 64
New ground 35
Number of inspirations 29, 135

o
Objective of the survey 101
Objectives 39, 46 f., 50, 52, 54, 60, 100, 102, 107, 118, 128, 133, 190 f.
– occupied with the past 53
OK stamp 84
Open Air festival 98
Open questions 54, 103, 146
Opinions Ideas 68
Optimisation 25, 68, 174, 181
Orchestration of the workshop 92
Organisational issues 92
Outsiders 14, 29, 34, 37, 42 ff., 47, 51, 58, 61, 64, 76, 92, 135, 177 f.
– and insiders 91, *see* insiders and outsiders
Overview 33, 118, 131, 156, 160, 162, 173, 175

Subject index | 207

P

Parameters for the successful generation of ideas 14
Participants 27, 45, 51-54, 59, 61, 64 f., 68 f., 72, 74 f., 78-94, 123-127, 129-133, 135, 137, 144, 156-162, 164 f., 168, 174-177, 179, 193
Participate 174
Participating in idea workshops 65
Payment 56, 61, 145, 175
People
– outsiders 61
– the right 29, 32, 55, 74, 155, 167, 180
People who always say "No" 85
ple who do preparation work nix
People who say "Mine" 60
People who think in the same way 57
People with no interest outside their own subject 70
People, interesting 29
PeopleManager 173 ff., 180
Perfectionism 92
Period of grace 171
Perspective
– extreme 63
– new 113
– unusual 168
– various 52, 83, 145
Pet food ideas 48, 110
Phases 26 ff., 37, 39, 45, 58, 74, 97, 116, 154, 174, 181, 183
Picking things up quickly 63
Picture of the machine 25, 28
Picture worlds 142
Pioneers 196
Planning ongoing 187
Plastic modelling material 86 f.
Polarisation 32, 106, 131, 160, 162, 164
Polarity 156
Portrayal of current reality 111
Possessive climate 60
Possessiveness 59 f., 69
Posters 89, 123, 152
Potential of ideas 154, 159 f., 165
Power of inspiration 22
PowerPoint 150 ff.
Practice field 47
Prejudices 43

Preparation 11, 45, 50, 54, 58, 78, 117, 119, 134, 155, 157, 162, 165 f., 175, 177
Presentation 33, 87, 106, 130, 137-143, 145-158, 161 f., 176 f.
– visual 142, 149, 150 ff.
Presentation forms 152
Principles
– of the industrial production of ideas 25, 79
– of mixing 61
– of optimization 68, 174, 181
– three 74
Priorities 57, 172, 188
Private individuals 43, 47-50
Procedure 26 f., 61, 69, 92, 97, 99, 122, 140, 154, 156, 160 f., 167
Process
– control 177
– defined 12 ff., 25
– democratic 159, 166
– industrial 36
– optimized 122
– standardized 12
– structured 13, 22, 25, 159
– predetermined 61
– part of 11, 61
– management, neutral 69 f.
Process management, neutral 69 f.
Product development 36, 119
Production 15, 21, 24 f., 27, 29, 30, 32, 34-37, 39, 41, 50, 71, 76, 79, 95, 97, 102, 109, 128, 134, 139, 141, 144, 171, 173 ff., 177 ff., 181, 186 ff., 196
Professionalism 12
Programme 63, 90 ff., 156, 159, 175, 186
Project
– briefing 33, 101
– countdown 190
– language 93
– manager 51, 68, 170
ProjectManager 157, 173 ff., 180, 187
ProjectOwner 28, 31, 33, 51, 134 f., 155
Projects
– complex 58, 88, 133
– sensitive 69
Prototyping 144

q
Quality
- assurance 178
- criteria 50
- monitoring 33
- of the working material 92
Quantity 27, 29 f., 121 f., 125, 127
Question formulation
- central 46
- idea generation 43, 79
- rudimentary 39
Questioning technique 103
Questionnaire Testing 104, 176
Questions
- positive 53
- stupid 42

r
Ranking list 156
Raw ideas 30, 73 f., 77, 97, 121, 175
Reading, further 195
Realists 189
Recommendation 106 f., 160, 165 f., 181
Repeat 26, 46, 51, 80, 190
Research and development 13, 24, 36, 41, 58
Researchers 99, 107
Resources 12, 33, 37, 112, 173 f., 183
Respect 64, 125, 168, 181
Retired people 107
Reward 69, 72, 112 f.
Reward system 12
Right of use 145
Risks 9 f., 58
Role 32, 70, 125, 149 f., 172, 174, 179 f., 187 f.
Role division in the IdeaTeam 172
Room 21, 45, 48, 74 ff., 80, 84, 92, 94, 116, 128, 130, 135, 146, 152, 158 f., 161, 180, 186
Rules for brainstorming 80
Rules of the game 11

s
Sample 98, 102, 105, 107, 176
Satisfaction 119, 180
Satisfaction rate 143
Scaled questions 103

Scenario 23, 25
Sceptical people 64
Scepticism 9, 178
School magazine 65, 67
School system 63
Scientists 57 f., 67
Search fields 52, 54
Searching for treasure 40
Secrecy 13, 72
Security 69, 99
Selection
- of interviewers 104
- of the idea 31 f., 154 f., 166, 183, 189
- of the survey group 97
Suitable 122
Selection of ideas 153 ff.
Selection process 155, 166
Selection process, disciplined 155
Self-presentation 141
Sender 138 f., 143
Show 63, 65, 90, 106 f., 110, 112, 134, 138, 146, 152, 156, 162, 164, 171, 183
Signposts 47
Sketches 83, 124, 148
Skills, technical 172
Small talk 90
Solving structure problems 119
Something to talk about 159
Sources of information 187
Specialist knowledge 134, 145, 168
Specialists 9, 24, 31, 55, 67 f., 72, 77, 98, 107, 120, 122, 132, 134
Speed 59, 64, 68, 80, 84, 90 f., 122, 125, 127, 141, 169, 181, 194
Spontaneous 93, 160
Standard deviation 156, 162, 164
Standstill 47, 174
Starting point 122
Stations 35, 82 ff., 115
Steward 92, 94
STOP-AIDS campaign 67
Strengths, personal 123
Stress 63, 72, 85, 169, 172
Structure and chaos 40
Structures 14, 36, 63, 119
Students 34, 70 ff., 196
Stumbling blocks 26
Style 134, 141–144, 149, 151
Subject clusters 116

Subject index | 209

Subject fields 41
Sub-questions 53 f.
Suggestions for improvement 96, 180
Support, technical 122
Survey Groups 95, 97, 106
- concepts 100 f., 176
- size 101

t
Taboos 41, 43
Talent 117, 145
Target groups 66 f, 98, 100 f., 104, 184 f.
- "young people" 98, 55
Target persons 96
Team
- colourful 122
- heterogeneous 65
- spirit 190
- work 172
Technique 9, 12, 23, 28, 34 f., 37, 64, 79, 94 f., 109 f., 115, 120, 123
Teenager 64, 78, 169
Testing and selecting interviewers 104
Tests 133, 174
Texts 117, 149, 169
Think about hierarchies 128
Thinking in compartments 9, 55, 58
Thinking, analytical 168
ThinkTank 41, 120 f., 123, 126, 132 ff., 174, 176, 187
ThinkTank Team 176
Threat 9
Tidiness 92
Time
- budgets 86
- pressure 64
- schedules 174, 181, 183
Tool bag 75
Tools 14, 25, 30, 32, 34 ff., 43, 50, 52, 79, 117, 121, 124, 148, 154, 167, 174 f., 179 f., 193
Top floor 185
Top management task 50
Trainees 70 f., 92, 137 f., 170
Transparency 32

Travel agency, on wheels 148
TrendBuy 115
TrendDescription 115 f.
TrendMag 115
TrendPhoto 115
TrendScouting 28, 30, 40, 53, 95, 109–121, 123, 174, 176
Tunnel vision 14

u
UMTS 26
Unaffected 62
Uneasiness 121
Unorthodox thinkers 61
Users 26, 29, 37, 70, 95 f., 100, 107

v
Validation of the favourite idea 97
Validation phase 32
Value chain 24
Ventilation 92
Video-beamer 80
Visualisation 140–144, 145, 147, 150
Visualisation form 145

w
WAP 26
Warm-up phase 64
Waste 23, 63 f., 76, 81, 155, 185
Watering-down 183
Web links 195
Welcome 113, 158, 159
Work techniques 90
Working materials for idea workshops 195
Worksheet 81, 84
Workshop language 93
Workshops, productive 168
Writer 124, 126 f., 170
Writing material 82, 86

y
Young people 34, 55 f., 61–68, 72, 77 ff., 87, 93, 96, 98 f., 107, 184 f.
Youth center 76